pocket
cornwall

GW00383645

Cornwall and the Cornish

Bernard Deacon

Welcome to
CORNWALL
KERNOW
a'gas dynergh

Alison Hodge

First published in 2010 by
Alison Hodge, 2 Clarence Place,
Penzance, Cornwall TR18 2QA, UK
info@alison-hodge.co.uk
www.alisonhodgepublishers.co.uk

© Bernard Deacon, 2010

Reprinted and updated 2014

The right of Bernard Deacon to be identified
as the author of this work has been asserted
by him in accordance with the Copyright,
Designs and Patents Act 1988.

ISBN-13 978-0-906720-72-1

British Library Cataloguing-in-Publication Data
A catalogue record for this book is available from
the British Library.

Designed and originated by
BDP – Book Development and Production,
Penzance, Cornwall

Printed in China

Title page: Sign by Greystone Bridge on entering
Cornwall over the River Tamar

Acknowledgements

Photographs are reproduced by kind permission of: Delabole Slate, page 23; ADG Fortescue, page 82; Alison Hodge, pages 9, 19, 24–5; Phil Hosken, page 28; Freya Laughton, page 101; Kim Laughton, pages 16, 28, 52–3, 104–5, 106 (L), 116–17; Phil Monckton, cover, page 107; NTPL/Aerial-Cam/Adam Stanford, pages 76–7; Skinner's Brewing Co., page 94; John Such, pages 65, 81. Photographs not otherwise attributed are by Christopher Laughton.

We are also grateful to the following for allowing us to take photographs: The Billy Bray Memorial Trust, pages 110, 111; Bodmin Jail, page 99; Caerhays Estate, pages 84, 85; The Eden Project, page 125; Franciscan Sisters of the Immaculate, pages 78, 79; Penlee House Gallery & Museum, Penzance, page 61; Philip Rowley, page 8; St Neot Parochial Church Council, pages 72, 73; St Swithin's Church, Launcells, pages 22, 35.

Contents

Narratives of Cornwall

Stithians Show (above). Cornish daffodils (left)

Cornwall contains no conurbation or large city, and to most UK residents, three-quarters of whom live in cities or their suburbs, it must seem relatively rustic. Small towns scattered through a landscape of little fields combine with distance from London to produce an impression that Cornwall is somehow deeply rural. It is true that farming has been an enduring feature of Cornwall's past. In the 1800s Cornish farmers largely gave up

Mevagissey (left). Newlyn (right)

the struggle to grow grain to concentrate on dairying and livestock. The railways brought new markets within reach after the 1850s, and farmers and horticulturists reaped the benefits of mild winters and early springs to sell their fruit, flowers and vegetables to a growing urban market.

Railways also allowed Cornwall's fishermen to send their fish more quickly to London, and in the later nineteenth century the fishing industry briefly boomed. This coincided with a rediscovery of Cornwall by artists and early tourists who, inaccurately, portrayed the fishing villages to a wider audience as timeless and quaint places. The stage was set for the mass tourism of the second half of the twentieth century. A fisherman may appear on the

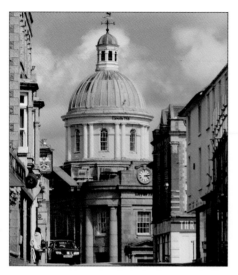 

A rural society interspersed with small towns: Penzance (above); Redruth (facing page)

traditional Cornish coat of arms but no farmer (or hotelier, come to that). In fact, fishermen and farmers were not the central players in the drama of Cornish history.

Two stories dominate Cornwall's past. The first is a tale of an economic rise and fall. Cornwall played a central role in the industrialization of the eighteenth and early nineteenth centuries. These were the years when the steam engine was developed to its highest level of efficiency by Cornish inventors and engineers. Population growth and mining created a dynamic industrial society in the west, bounded roughly by the towns of Truro, Falmouth, Helston and Penzance and with its epicentre in the mining towns of Camborne and Redruth. Yet this industrial society did not spawn the large cities that became a feature of later industrial regions in the north of England and Scotland. It remained a rural society, interspersed with small towns.

Growth was cut short by falls in the prices of copper, lead and tin after 1866. Ironically, this was partly the result of Cornish

miners' efforts as they helped to open up new mining frontiers in the Americas and Australia – sources of metal that were to out-produce the older and deeper mines of Cornwall. One of Europe's first industrial regions was soon transformed into one of its first de-industrialized regions. Cornwall's mining society withered after the 1870s, confined to a shrinking heartland centred on the towns of Camborne and Redruth.

For some, this produced social and cultural paralysis. During the late nineteenth and early twentieth centuries Cornwall seemed to stagnate. Its population declined, bled by the emigration of the more adventurous. Its people looked inwards and backwards for reassurance, mired in nostalgia and settling for the familiar and the familial, resisting change and dreaming of the good old days. But this picture of a backward Cornwall stuck in the past has been overdrawn, missing continuing signs of dynamism and underplaying a persisting and confident sense of place.

Part of that confidence owed its genesis to a second story. This was a narrative that, although gaining in influence after the 1860s, looked back much further to Cornwall's pre-industrial past. Cornwall's origins were not those of an English county. Instead its roots lay in a British Britain, long before the arrival of the English. The Cornish language was a standing reminder, well into the 1700s and even now inescapably present in place-names, that the Cornish were different. Other 'Celtic' aspects could be cited. For example, a special affection for King Arthur was evident. This had led to a punch-up in Bodmin in the 1100s. A visiting group of French canons had to contend with an irate local who took exception to their airy dismissal of the prediction of Arthur's inevitable return. When Arthurian romances became

St Piran's Day parade (left). Penzance Town Crier, Philip (Piglet) Rowley (right)

fashionable in the twelfth century, the literate classes were reminded of their British and non-English origins.

Later, when historians wrote their histories of Cornwall in the eighteenth and nineteenth centuries, they rediscovered these non-English origins, and a history that included violent struggles against the Saxons. All this fuelled a narrative that built on an earlier popular self-identification as 'ancient Britons', and re-invented the Cornish as 'Celts'. From this emerged a revivalist movement. Antiquarians hunted out scraps of the Cornish language, and enthusiasts set about restoring a revived medieval version of the language. In the twentieth century the Revival busied itself with inventing the symbols of Celtic Cornwall – a Gorseth of blue-robed bards,

Annual Open Gorseth ceremony, St Just, 1982. The Awen, representing Love, Justice and Truth, features on the banner carried in procession (left). Bards James Hodge and Valerie Jacob (above). The blue of the robes represents the sky; black and gold the colours of the ancient Cornish kings

a flag, a tartan and a kilt – the paraphernalia any self-respecting Celt would need. All this guaranteed that Cornwall would remain, according to the archaeologist Bryan Ward-Perkins, 'the one part of England where not all indigenous inhabitants automatically describe themselves as "English".'

The first narrative – of industrial rise and fall – underpinned Cornish pride and self-confidence. As Herman Merivale, a percipient temporary resident and lawyer, wrote in the 1850s, the Cornish were 'considerably self-opinionated… the thorough Cornishman's respect for his shrewdness and that of his clan is unbounded, or only equalled by his profound contempt for "foreigners" from the east… the feeling increases ludicrously in intensity as we advance further west.' On its own this intense local patriotism could co-exist with a wider loyalty to England. However, the second narrative differentiates Cornwall more obviously from England, and reminds the Cornish of their separate origins. Within this narrative, to be Cornish is to be something other than English.

Crowns Engine Houses

The story of mining runs like a counterpoint in Cornwall's past, its rise and fall accompanying the dramatic symphony of the Cornish people toiling to win a living from their land. The land itself may not have been that productive, but underneath were untold mineral riches. At its height – in the 1800s – mining provided the rhythm to which the whole Cornish economy moved. At other times, for example the early 1900s, the mines were

the visible expression of a harsh dissonance as the industry collapsed, threatening to drag down the Cornish economy in its wake.

Tin was first won in eastern Cornwall, high on the slopes of Bodmin Moor and Hensbarrow, from the streams washing tin ores down from the moors. Stream works were joined by tunnels and underground working as early as the 1400s as miners began to pursue the lodes underground. By the 1700s mines such as Polgooth, near St Austell, or Poldice in Gwennap were up to 600 ft (183 m) deep and ranked among the largest industrial enterprises in Britain. At the same time a rising demand from brass manufacturers for copper triggered the hunt for that mineral. Copper mining created one of Europe's first industrial regions in west Cornwall.

As copper mining enjoyed its century and a half of growth, mines were opened across the length and breadth of Cornwall, from over the border near Tavistock to here at Botallack, near St Just. The spectacularly located Crowns engine houses, the lower built in 1835 and the upper in 1862, served an inclined shaft that ran out under the ocean. Miners worked under the sea, sometimes, according to contemporary tales, hearing the boulders rumbling along the sea bed above them.

Wheal Peevor

Wheal Peevor, to the north-east of Redruth, was never one of Cornwall's major mines. But its surface remains provide us with by far the best picture of a later nineteenth-century working mine site. During a short-lived tin boom in 1871–2 Wheal Peevor was re-opened and new engine houses built. These housed the steam engines that had three main functions – driving pumps, whims (winching engines) and stamps. All three of these can be seen here. In the biggest mines

there would also be man engines – a kind of moving ladder which the miners used to get to and from the mine workings.

Pumping engines required the biggest buildings: they worked the pumps which drained water from the mines. Whim engines powered the raising or lowering of kib-bles (buckets) carrying material into and out of the depths. Finally, stamps engines drove the stamps that crushed the ore brought to surface through the whim shafts. This was prior to its 'dressing' by an army of young women (bal maidens) and children. These swarmed across the dressing floors on the

surface wielding various-sized hammers to break the ore from the waste rock, or tended the buddles used in separating the tin.

The majority of an estimated 250 or more engine houses that still stood in the mid-twentieth century have now disappeared, collapsed and disused, deliberately robbed for their stones, or replaced by industrial estates. It's therefore rare for a mine site to contain examples of all the major types of engine house. Peevor, restored and made more accessible to the public in 2007, provides the best reminder of what a working Cornish mine looked like. Its most productive period was squeezed into a few years between 1875 and 1883, when a maximum of around 190 underground miners and 140 surface workers could be found here.

Conserved remains of buddles (facing page)

South Crofty

South Crofty, at Pool, was a relatively insignificant mine during the heyday of mining in the mid-1800s, dwarfed by its neighbour to the west, Dolcoath, the queen of Cornish mines and the most productive mine of the nineteenth century. But Dolcoath succumbed to the post-war depression of the early 1920s, and later Crofty took over its workings along with those of other neighbouring mines in the aptly named 'central mining district'.

Perhaps Crofty will go down in history as the last working mine in Cornwall. 'Perhaps' as plans remained to re-open the mine for producing tin. However, these were successively postponed as the neighbouring land began to be transformed into the Heartlands visitor attraction plus housing estates.

In the 1980s a handful of mines were still operating in Cornwall, including a few – Wheal Jane and Mount Wellington and Pendarves mines – which had reopened as tin prices rose enticingly in the 1970s. But what goes up must come down, and consecutive collapses in metal prices in the 1980s and '90s decimated what was left of the mining industry in Cornwall. First the new mines closed, to be followed by Geevor at Pendeen, leaving the isolated community there with no obvious means of subsistence. Then in 1998 even Crofty, the richest of the remaining mines, could struggle on no longer.

The despair this evoked was deeper than that accompanying normal bad economic news. Local communities mourned the end of over 2,000 years of mining. Brass bands led emotional processions of people from Camborne and Redruth, who converged on the mine to pay their respects and say their goodbyes. With the apparent death of deep mining something seemed to have been ripped out of the heart of Cornwall, and the sense of loss was tangible. However, perhaps the grief was premature and mining, like Cornwall itself, still has the ability to rise like a phoenix.

Someone painted a message on the walls of Crofty after it closed: 'Cornish lads are fishermen, and Cornish lads are miners too, but when the fish and tin are gone what are the Cornish boys to do?' This perhaps struck the right note of nostalgic poignancy, but the implied economic structure would have been out of date in the 1930s, let alone the 1990s. The answer is simple – Cornish boys, and girls, work in service industries, especially local government, education and the health sector, which are the biggest employers of labour in modern Cornwall.

Lamorna Granite

Cornwall's central spine is made up of four granite outcrops, from Bodmin Moor in the east through Hensbarrow and Carnmenellis to West Penwith at the Land's End. It is said that every Cornish person also has a granite core. Easy-going on the surface, we can be obstinate and unmovable if pushed too far.

Cornishmen combined with Cornish granite in the heyday of the industry in the 1800s. Cornwall's granite stone provided the building material for some of Victorian Britain's major construction projects, including docks, dockyards, forts, lighthouses and Westminster Bridge. Granite was also exported overseas for civil engineering projects in continental Europe, South Africa, India and Argentina. Granite had been used for millennia. In prehistory standing stones were rough-hewn from granite, and in the medieval period Cornish churches and bridges were built with it. In those days granite stones were just picked up from the surface of the moors, these 'moorstones' being cut by stonemasons. By the 1820s quarries began to appear, and from the 1840s granite quarrying enjoyed a half-century of boom.

The busiest quarrying district was near Penryn, which became the centre of the granite trade. Other quarrying areas were more remote, either on high moors well away from the ports or with no safe harbour nearby. The Land's End quarries fell into the latter category. Lamorna and other quarries in that area were developed after 1849. At first a small jetty was used here for loading the stone, but hazardous sea conditions led to its abandonment and granite blocks were carried to Penzance for shipment.

At its peak perhaps as many as 2,000 men were employed in and around granite quarries across the length and breadth of Cornwall. However, although the industry escaped the slump which devastated Cornish mining in the 1870s, after the 1890s it went the same way. Unable to compete with cheaper Scandinavian granite, wages were cut, quarries closed, and quarrymen emigrated. Rusting traces of cranes and railway lines and the heaps of discarded quarry waste were left to bear evocative witness to this once-flourishing industry.

Lamorna Cove, 2014. The former quarry and heaps of granite are returning to nature; the pier is crumbling, damaged by storms (facing page)

Clay Tips

The first motorized tourists venturing down the A30 across Goss Moor on a sunny day may have been puzzled by the sight of a range of sparkling white pyramids to the south. These were the 'Cornish Alps' – until the 1960s conical-shaped piles of waste thrown up by the china clay industry. After the Aberfan disaster in Wales the clay tips were flattened for safety reasons, and took on their more prosaic modern shape.

This industry has been strangely marginal to Cornish life. Although in the nineteenth century shafts were sunk into clay ground and tunnels dug, clay is now extracted by a process of open-cast mining. For Cornish historians such as AK Hamilton Jenkin in the 1920s and '30s, the clay labourer wielding his shovel in the open air struck a less romantic figure than the underground miner, seeking ore by the dim light of a guttering candle. The clay industry was also relatively new, and did not enjoy all the ancient historical associations of metal mining.

Yet, like metal mining, the clay industry was a primary industry based on the export of a natural resource. Like mining it provided the raw materials for secondary industries else-where. Even more than mining, it ripped up the landscape and left acres of desolate spoil heaps. As with mining, a few made vast profits and became very rich while the majority made do on a bare minimum, finding consolation in their chapels and the fabric of local community and family life.

Clay was first discovered in Cornwall in the west, at Tregonning Hill in the 1740s, but clay pits began to be opened on Hensbarrow, to the north of St Austell, from the 1770s. This small district went on to produce 90 per cent of all the clay extracted in Britain. The clay industry's boom days came in the early twentieth century, production increasing more than ten-fold between 1858 and 1910, and rising rapidly again in the period following the Second World War after difficult times during the depression of the inter-war years.

As well as adding to the uniqueness of the Cornish landscape, the clay industry produced its own tough and resourceful communities. Furthermore, clay workers were prepared to struggle for their rights and for a decent standard of living. They were among the first groups of working men in Cornwall to form trade unions. A bitter strike in 1913 to secure union recognition and an increase in the 18 shillings (80 pence) a week wage became a part of local lore.

Clay tips (top). The fabric of local community: Whitemoor (above left) and Roche (above right)

A window into the life of the inter-war clay communities is opened by Jack Clemo's *Autobiography of a Rebel* and his novel *Wilding Graft*. The clay country has for some reason produced more writers and novelists than other parts of Cornwall, from the Hocking brothers (and a sister) in the early twentieth century, who wrote hundreds of novels between them, to Alan Kent, the prolific contemporary author of gritty books like *Proper Job, Charlie Curnow!*

Delabole Slate Quarry

Hidden in Delabole on the bleak north Cornish plateau is what is reputedly the largest hole in Europe. Delabole quarry, between the settlements of Pengelly and Medrose,

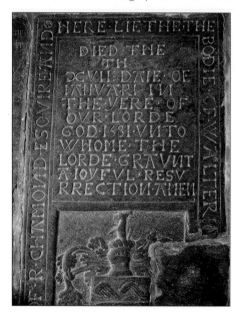

A slate memorial in Launcells church (above); the quarry (facing page, top); slate hanging on old houses in Grampound, and on a new extension at Newlyn Art Gallery (facing page left and right)

has been the site of slate working since at least the fourteenth century. From the 1100s there are records of slate being used for roofing, and by the 1300s mentions of slate quarries in Cornwall, including Delabole.

What were originally a number of small, separate works gradually amalgamated and consolidated themselves into one huge quarry. A painting by Thomas Rowlandson in 1808 shows an already deep pit with water wheels and horse-powered engines, men working on cutting the slates, and horses and carts waiting to remove them. It is likely that the quarry had expanded rapidly in the later eighteenth century as town growth and industrialization boosted the demand for slate.

By the mid-nineteenth century Delabole quarry, along with others in east Cornwall, was second in Britain only to the slate district of north Wales. Unlike north Wales, however, slate has been continuously extracted from Delabole, although now only a handful of workers produce the same amount as hundreds did in the 1800s. While the number employed has inevitably contracted, the village of Delabole remains. Like mining villages further south and west – Pensilva, Darite, Four Lanes, Leedstown and Pendeen, for example – it is a living memorial to Cornwall's rural-industrial heritage.

Harveys of Hayle

As the number of mines grew between the early 1700s and the 1850s there was a voracious demand for engines, engine boilers and pitwork. This was largely met from within Cornwall, from the foundries that sprang up from the later 1700s. For example, Perran Foundry was started on the banks of the creek at Perranarworthal, financed by the Foxes of Falmouth in 1791. Later, it was joined by foundries at St Blazey, Charlestown, St Just, Tuckingmill, Redruth and other places.

Meanwhile Holmans, opening its Camborne works in 1839, grew into Cornwall's principal twentieth-century engineering firm, employing over 2,000 people at its peak and keeping Camborne's heart beating. A large part of the former Holmans site is now occupied by a Tesco superstore – a telling shift in priorities from production to consumption.

However, two of the largest Cornish foundries co-existed in the same town, Hayle, which produced 80 per cent of the world's steam pumping engines. Copperhouse Foundry started as a copper smelting works in the 1750s, before succumbing around 1810 to competition from south Welsh copper smelters. These were located more conveniently close to the coalfield and financed, ironically, mainly by Cornish capital after the 1800s.

The Cornish Copper Company, which ran Copperhouse, in the east of the straggling town of Hayle, faced a bitter rival at the other end of the settlement – the family firm of Harveys. Between the 1810s and the 1860s Harveys employed over a thousand men and boys, and produced engine boilers not only for Cornish mines but for mines and other engineering projects across the globe.

In 1869 Copperhouse fell victim to the economic storm beginning to engulf Cornish mines, although Harveys struggled on into the twentieth century. Its foundry closed in 1903, but the firm survived as builders' merchants into the 1960s. Much of the once-dominating foundry works was demolished, although various buildings remain. Sadly, really informative interpretation signage is lacking, although the Hayle Heritage Centre is a welcome addition to the site.

Some of the buildings that made up Harvey's Foundry. Redevelopment by Harvey's Foundry Trust includes craft workshops (top right). A painting by Clive Carter (facing page)

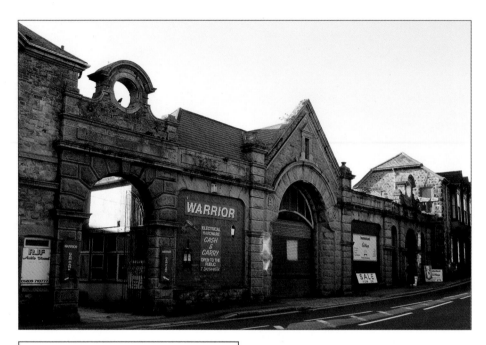

Tuckingmill Fuseworks

By the 1600s tin miners were probing deeper and further in their search for the 'white gold' – tin ore. To reach ore-bearing ground they had to cut shafts and tunnels (known as levels). Before the late 1600s ground was won and ore was extracted entirely by labour power. When the rock was hard, progress was pitifully slow as miners hacked away with pick and shovel.

The introduction of gunpowder – the first example supposedly in Gwinear in the 1670s – greatly speeded this up. Powder was used in a series of controlled – or often uncontrolled – explosions that advanced the rock face. The main problem of using gunpowder was in providing a fuse that could allow the miner to light it and retire to a safe distance.

Primitive methods using goose quills and other devices to carry a trail of powder produced short and unreliable fuses. In consequence, accidents were all too common. The first of many deaths from explosions was recorded in Breage parish register in 1689.

Nonetheless, gunpowder became an essential part of mining as the number of mines grew rapidly in the 1700s. By the early 1800s powder mills had been started, usually in out-of-the-way woods, to supply this need. But the appalling scale of accidents from premature explosions pricked the con-

sciences of many and, belatedly, attention turned to designing a safer fuse. William Bickford (1774–1834), a staunch Methodist, hit on the idea of twisting powder into a rope after visiting a friend's ropeworks, and the safety fuse was invented in 1831.

Bickford's works at Tuckingmill, in the heart of the central mining district, became the centre of a Cornish fuse industry that dominated world markets until the invention of dynamite and electrical fuses in the twentieth century. But even when technology moved on Cornwall played a role – dynamite works were established at Upton Towans near Hayle in the 1900s. Within less than a decade they were the scene of a disastrous explosion that was reportedly audible ten miles away in Redruth.

Richard Trevithick

Replica of Trevithick's 1801 locomotive, built by members of the Trevithick Society, 2001

For a few years in the late eighteenth century a small district bounded by Redruth, Camborne and Falmouth was home to three men – William Murdoch, Thomas Macadam and Richard Trevithick – who played a key role in inventing the technology that made the modern world. They remind us that Cornwall was a powerhouse of the industrial revolution.

Only one was Cornish. Richard Trevithick (1771–1833), the flawed genius from Pool, is best known for developing the steam engine, one of which went 'up Camborne Hill', leaving that town with a memorable song, *Going up Camborne Hill, coming down*. The voracious appetite of the copper mines for expensive Welsh coal to feed the growing host of steam engines stimulated a constant search for greater efficiency. A number of 'pirate' engines were produced, even while the patent monopoly of James Watt and Matthew Boulton still ran before 1800.

One of the most effective was the high-pressure steam engine developed in Cornwall's mining heartland by Trevithick. But he did not stop at improving the steam engine, going on to invent the world's first successful self-propelled passenger-carrying road locomotive in 1801, and the first railway engine in 1804. Physically a large and dominating presence, Trevithick also possessed a mercurial temperament. Applying his energies to a number of projects, he was notoriously poor in managing men and finances. In 1816 he went to South America – Peru and Colombia – before returning, penniless, ten years later.

However, Trevithick had established himself as the hero of Cornwall's industrial revolution – the great inventor, unconstrained by lesser, more mundane matters, too impatient to suffer fools gladly. Something in his per-

sonality appealed to the Cornish. Although at the time his death in 1833 went relatively unnoticed, he was later memorialized in a statue outside Camborne Public Library. The annual Trevithick Day celebrations in Camborne recognize his place in the town's history.

Murdoch House

William Murdoch (1754–1839) was a Scot from Ayrshire who was employed by the Birmingham-based partnership of Boulton & Watt in the 1780s as an engineer in Cornwall. Boulton & Watt at this time held a lucrative patent on the steam engine, and as a result had erected a number of engines in Cornwall. Soon Murdoch was put in charge of all these. However, he was not just a gifted engineer but had interests beyond the steam engine.

It was in this modest house in the centre of Redruth in 1792 that Murdoch first used coal gas to fuel a lamp, thus inventing the gas lighting which was to become universal during the nineteenth century. Redruth was the obvious base for a man whose job took him to many of the mines of Cornwall. In the late eighteenth century the town was centrally placed in the copper district that stretched from Gwinear to Gwennap, and not inconvenient for the further-flung tin mines.

In the medieval period Redruth was a nondescript market town a mile distant from its church, serving an under-populated district of open, uncultivated downland and poor agricultural land. By 1801 it had become one of the largest towns in Cornwall, with a parish population of almost 5,000, of whom perhaps 3,000 lived in the town. This made it the most populous parish in Cornwall. Only Falmouth (with 3,700 residents) and possibly Truro were larger towns. Redruth was Cornwall's industrial town, rough and ready but dynamic and bustling. It was a place that attracted men of creative energy like Murdoch, along with a growing class of labourers and their families dependent on the mines for their livelihood as well as enterprising shopkeepers and traders who kept this restless population provisioned.

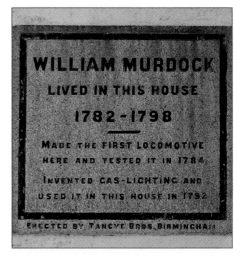

WILLIAM MURDOCK
LIVED IN THIS HOUSE
1782-1798

MADE THE FIRST LOCOMOTIVE HERE AND TESTED IT IN 1784
INVENTED GAS-LIGHTING AND USED IT IN THIS HOUSE IN 1792

ERECTED BY TANGYE BROS, BIRMINGHAM

Humphry Davy

If Trevithick represents the heroic inventor who, through his individual efforts, symbolizes the achievements of Cornwall's classic industrial period, then Humphry Davy represents the more sober side of the story.

It is now argued that the greatest advances in the efficiency of the steam engine stemmed from small-scale improvements made by working engineers and engine men at the mines, and were not the result of spectacular breakthroughs by brilliant inventors. From around 1810 to 1840 the efficiency of the steam engine in Cornwall advanced by leaps and bounds. This was a consequence of the day-to-day tinkering of an army of engineers whose names are now largely forgotten. Their collective effort comprises the real heroism of the Cornish industrial revolution. In those years engineers improved the steam engine to a level that contemporary scientists had insisted was impossible.

If one side of the inventive coin was the practical working engineer, the other was the culture of scientific endeavour that flowered in the early years of the nineteenth century. Humphry Davy (1778–1829) arose out of this inquisitive and rational culture.

From relatively humble beginnings in Penzance, Davy was apprenticed to a surgeon and took up chemistry. This was no idle hobby, and in his day he was the leading writer and lecturer in the subject. He gave addresses to the Royal Society in London, and was feted by the intellectuals of Paris. In recognition of his work he was knighted in 1812.

His statue looks down over Market Jew Street in Penzance, reminding us of this son of Cornwall who played such a leading role in the intellectual ferment of the early nineteenth century. Ironically, Davy's best-known invention – the miners' safety lamp – was a boon to coal miners rather than metal miners. It was largely irrelevant in Cornish mines where combustible air and underground gas explosions were not a major hazard. Miners here continued to take candles underground for lighting until the early 1900s.

Goldsworthy Gurney

Goldsworthy Gurney was born Henry Lovell Goldsworthy Gurney in 1793, near Padstow. Like Humphry Davy, he trained as a surgeon, practising in Wadebridge, a few miles from his birthplace. Like Davy, he moved to London and also became a lecturer in chemistry. But Gurney was badly bitten by the inventing bug, linked to a chance meeting when a schoolboy with the great Richard Trevithick.

In 1825 he copied Trevithick by inventing a steam carriage. More successful than his mentor, this seemed to be a practical means of road transport, despite the ever-present danger of the boiler exploding. Unfortunately for Gurney, it came to nothing in the face of opposition from the horse-drawn transport lobby and prohibitive tolls on steam road vehicles. Gurney moved back to Cornwall in 1831, and settled at the small resort of Bude, where he built Bude Castle near the beach, close to the canal that had been cut in 1823 to take sand and lime to farmers inland.

In the 1820s Gurney had improved on oil lamps and candles by inventing limelight, adding lime and magnesia to an oxyhydrogen blowpipe to produce a brilliant light. This became widely used in theatres – hence the modern meaning of 'limelight'. Back in Cornwall Gurney followed this up with 'Bude Light'. This introduced oxygen to an oil-lamp flame to give a more intense light, which he then ingeniously transmitted around his home via a number of mirrors.

In the 1850s Gurney devised a ventilation and heating system for the new Houses of Parliament, where the members were complaining of the fetid stench that permeated the chamber. In those days it was caused by nothing more than a press of bodies and a lack of ventilation. Gurney installed a new furnace and a system to circulate air, and added his lighting to illuminate the dark recesses of the place.

For this he was knighted in 1863. Soon after he suffered a stroke, spending his last years at home in Cornwall. Gurney was buried in 1875 at the peaceful Launcells church, close to the upper reaches of the Tamar.

Bude Canal (facing page). Bude Castle (top). St Swithin's Church, Launcells (above)

Royal Cornwall Polytechnic Society

In 1814 Cornwall's first literary institution – the Cornwall Geological Society – had begun to meet in Penzance. It was followed in 1818 by the Cornwall Philosophical Society (later the Royal Institution of Cornwall) in Truro. Not to be outdone, Falmouth followed suit in 1833 with its Cornwall Polytechnic Society – purportedly the idea of 17-year-old Anna Maria Fox. Anna was a member of Falmouth's leading family, whose country houses such as Trebah and Carwinion lie scattered across

The Customs House (left) and synagogue (right)

the countryside to the west of Falmouth. Although other towns set up their own literary institutes, these first three were a cut above the rest. The only ones later to attain the sought-after 'royal' prefix, they claimed to be societies for the whole of Cornwall rather than a mere locality.

Their character also reflected Cornwall's industrial history. The first in Penzance specialized in geology and mineral specimens, the basis for Cornwall's mining industry. While the Royal Institution of Cornwall more closely aped literary institutions in English towns and cities, the Polytechnic Society had from the start a strongly practical bent. For instance, it offered a reward for a device that would end the necessity of miners climbing up and down ladders to and from their places

of work – an increasingly exhausting finale to the working day as mines got ever deeper. This stimulated the invention by Michael Loam of the man engine, first installed at Tresavean Mine near Lanner in 1842.

The Polytechnic had a commanding physical presence, unlike the other institutions; the Royal Institution did not move into its new purpose-built museum in River Street, Truro until 1919. The Polytechnic's Greek Doric building in Church Street was one of a series of imposing buildings erected in Falmouth from the 1810s onwards as the town prospered from its association with the Packet service. As well as the Polytechnic, these included the Customs House, the Classical and Mathematical School, the Royal Hotel and a synagogue for one of Cornwall's two small Jewish communities.

Portreath Harbour

As the production of copper from the central mining district around Camborne and Redruth soared in the eighteenth century, local mine investors and landlords were confronted by transport bottlenecks. It was increasingly difficult to import enough coal to feed the growing number of steam engines, or to export the copper ore quickly and cheaply. The north coast offered few harbours for shipping between Hayle, with its treacherous sand bar, and Padstow, which was too remote from the mines.

The Bassets of Tehidy owned most of the coastline north of Camborne-Redruth, and here they encouraged the development of Basset's Cove, or Portreath, as a port for the mining district. Construction of a pier began in 1760, and work on the harbour continued intermittently until 1846. The small harbour provided some shelter for ships. But on a stormy day when the wind blows from the north, you can appreciate the seamanship required for mariners to gain its safety. Indeed, the harbour could be closed for days on end due to adverse weather – one of the reasons why Portreath was eventually eclipsed by south-coast ports in the nineteenth century.

Another problem facing the mine owners was how to move the heavy coal and ore overland to and from the mines. Long trains of mules were the traditional answer, but by the early nineteenth century these were not only churning up the primitive lanes and roads of west Cornwall but costing a fortune in fodder at a time of inflated grain prices. The obvious solution was rail. Cornwall's first horse-drawn tramway was built between Portreath and the St Day mines in the decade from 1809 to 1819. Later, a branch of the main railway line was built to Portreath, connected by an impressive incline, up and down which trucks were hauled by a stationary engine. Unfortunately, the lower end of this has been thoroughly obscured by housing development as Portreath's income now comes from tourism rather than trading.

Treffry Viaduct

The dignified Treffry Viaduct soars 90 ft (27 m) above the Luxulyan Valley, a product of mid-Cornwall's industrialization, which moved up a gear in the 1810s. In that decade rich deposits of copper ore were discovered to the east of St Austell around St Blazey and Par. At about the same time farmers were beginning to dig small china clay pits in the uplands of Hensbarrow Downs, while local miners pursued the tin lodes underground.

All this extra activity needed better transport or it was in danger of being stifled at birth. Joseph Thomas Austen, better known as Joseph Treffry (1782–1850) of Place House in Fowey was the driving force behind much of the improved transport infrastructure of early Victorian mid-Cornwall. Treffry, the principal investor in the rich Fowey Consols copper mine, dreamt of harbours at Par and Newquay and a network of canals and tramways linking these to the remote yet clay- and ore-rich uplands.

His viaduct at Luxulyan – the first large granite viaduct in Cornwall – was built between 1839 and 1842 to carry a tramway across the deep valley and ease the problems of bringing mineral produce down to the coast. The viaduct also carried a leat, which ingeniously powered an incline to transfer trucks to the head of a canal from Par.

The railway and canal stimulated the growth of Par docks, Cornwall's major outlet for clay during the twentieth century, its 'dries' dominating Par beach. The chimneys with their plumes of steam were for decades the major feature of this area, reminders of the industry that lay behind the landscape.

Charlestown

Charlestown is a creation of Cornwall's industrial revolution. In 1790 this hamlet overlooking West Polmear beach boasted a mere nine inhabitants. By 1801, 281 resided in the new, bustling port of Charlestown. Work began in 1791 on a pier, lock gates and warehouses as the harbour was built on land owned by the Rashleighs of nearby Mena-billy House. Charles Rashleigh gave his name to the new settlement (and to the village of Mount Charles just to the east of St Austell).

As clay production and local copper and tin output grew after 1810, this small port enjoyed a generation-long boom. Sailing vessels packed its harbour loading clay and ore, and delivering much-needed coal for domestic and industrial use. After the 1840s other, bigger ports, notably Par and Fowey, were developed, leaving Charlestown to sink into a dignified decline. It is now once more home to sailing ships; several are berthed here and are in demand for period films.

Global Communications

In the early 1960s the dishes of Goonhilly Satellite Earth Station added a new yet rapidly familiar dimension to the Cornish landscape. Their position on 65 hectares of the flat plateau of the Lizard peninsula made them unmissable from many miles around.

The juxtaposition of the radically new with extremely old relics of former times somehow made for perfect harmony. The dishes – the first built to receive the path-breaking television images bounced across the Atlantic via Telstar in 1962 – were not the direct result of home-grown Cornish ingenuity. Yet they seemed to encapsulate the tradition of being at the cutting edge of technology that had been proudly fostered in Cornwall since the eighteenth century.

Goonhilly was the latest in a succession of undervalued Cornish-based contributions to the history of modern communications. In 1870 the small cove of Porthcurno in West Penwith became the landing point for a telegraph cable to India. Porthcurno was chosen because of its remoteness and the lack of shipping that might damage the submarine cables with their anchors. From this beginning, Cornwall became a vital link in the chain of imperial connections that held the British Empire together. At its peak in 1928, 14 telegraph cables were operating at Porthcurno

– the world's largest cable station at the hub of a global communications network.

Back on the windswept peninsula of the Lizard, the first radio signals had been sent across the Atlantic in December 1901 from Poldhu near Mullion to Guglielmo Marconi in Newfoundland. Marconi's Wireless Telegraph Company and the Eastern Telegraph Company which ran Porthcurno merged in 1928, and in 1934 became Cable & Wireless. Porthcurno housed Cable & Wireless's training college until 1993, although the telegraph cables had stopped carrying their global messages in the 1960s as telephone replaced telegraph. As the century of telegraph faded into history, television took over.

For a generation or so the futuristic dishes pointed to the stars as they decoded the messages in the microwaves that silently and invisibly created the global village. But they proved much less permanent than the Bronze Age burial mounds and menhirs around them.

In 2006 it was announced that Goonhilly would no longer be used and all but the Grade II listed original dish would be gradually dismantled. Goonhilly's future lay in tourism, with its visitor centre telling the story of modern telecommunications. This was put on hold in 2011 when the site was acquired by Goonhilly Earth Station Ltd, who plan

Marconi aerial (top) and monument (above). Goonhilly dishes (facing page)

'space sector growth opportunities'. Meanwhile, the nearby wind turbines provide an interesting backdrop to the satellite dishes. From technological cutting edge to cultural tourism and green energy in many ways sums up the story of modern Cornwall.

Hawker's Hut

In this hut at Morwenstow, made of timbers washed up by the sea, Robert Stephen Hawker (1803–75), Vicar of Morwenstow from 1834 until his death, sat and mused and composed his works. On the high cliffs looking out over the watery desert in front of him, Hawker dreamt of romantic times before industrialization, mining and – even more terrible – Methodism, blighted the land.

But one composition that did not see its inception in this remote spot was *Trelawny*, or *The Song of the Western Men*. Hawker wrote this in 1826, restoring scraps of seventeenth-century songs to celebrate Sir Jonathan Trelawny (1650–1721), Cornishman and Bishop of Bristol. Trelawny was one of seven bishops incarcerated in the Tower of London in 1687 for opposing James II's attempts to give more toleration to Catholics and Nonconformists.

Trelawny's staunch defence of the Established Church appealed to the young Hawker's romantic Toryism. He cleverly linked this to an almost forgotten tradition of Cornish rebelliousness. But in doing so he helped to invert its meaning. From protesting violently against the ruling dynasty or the religious reforms creating the Church of England,

Hawker completed the job of transforming the Cornish into loyal defenders of the Protestant Church. This image had already supplanted and tamed earlier Cornish intransigence after the seventeenth-century civil wars. The remarkable thing about *Trelawny* is how quickly it became a de-facto national anthem. By the 1850s it was being described as a 'soul stirring favourite and patriotic song', while Bishop Trelawny was regarded as a 'demigod' on a par with King Arthur.

However, although *Trelawny* has a central place in Cornish culture, Hawker was a marginal figure in nineteenth-century Cornwall. Born in Plymouth, vicar of a border parish on the far northern extremity of the land, High Church (he converted to Catholicism on his deathbed) and romantically reactionary, Hawker's view of John Wesley would not have endeared him to the mass of the Cornish, although it contained more than a grain of truth. Hawker wrote that John Wesley 'found the miners and fishermen an upstanding, rollicking, courageous people, he left them a downlooking, lying, selfish-hearted throng.'

Hawker's Hut (top); Morwenstow's Church of St Morwenna and St John the Baptist (bottom left); the view from the cliffs by the Hut (bottom right)

Discovering Difference

Bishop Benson was the first Bishop of the new Truro diocese. In the 1880s he wrote, rather wearily one suspects, that the Cornish never tired of telling him how 'different' they were. A more recent Bishop of Truro, after being forcibly informed of the slaughter that accompanied the Prayer Book rising of 1549, felt it necessary to apologize for the misdeeds of his church half a millennium before. He was, he said in 2007, 'sorry about what happened and I think it was an enormous mistake.'

Both bishops were reacting to the Cornish desire to be different. In the nineteenth century difference began to be actively sought out everywhere – in occupations, superstitions, beliefs. Once under way, the hunt for difference continued unabated into the 1900s, from the deliberate symbol-building of the revivalists to the marketing gurus of the Great Western Railway who invented the Cornish Riviera. A desperate urge to be different gained momentum in the second half of the twentieth century, as it was feared Cornwall was fast becoming indistinguishable from anywhere else.

While some differences are sheer romantic fiction, others have endured for centuries: the language, the border and the Duchy.

The Cornish language was and is a crucially important marker of difference. Up to the end of the eighteenth century the Cornish spoke a language that wasn't English. Or some did. Opinions vary as to when people in east Cornwall adopted the conquerors' tongue in preference to Cornish. Both surname and place-name evidence strongly suggest a date for language loss before the mid-1300s. This early demise of Cornish in the east, coupled with its resilience in the west for another two to four hundred years afterwards resulted in an enduring difference *within* Cornwall.

The second marker of difference is both physical and at the same time imagined. Cornwall is surrounded on three sides by the sea, and on the fourth the River Tamar is its border for the majority of its length. The Tamar therefore takes on symbolic attributes as the frontier between two peoples or nations or counties, depending on one's preference. So, for many generations crossing the Tamar has been invested with a symbolism

The 'Cornish Riviera': the Great Western Hotel, Newquay (left). Subtropical Cordyline australis *(right)*

that is to many much deeper than merely crossing an inconvenient stretch of water.

A third marker of difference is the presence of historic institutions such as the Duchy of Cornwall, constructed out of the older earldom in 1337, or the Stannaries, with their courts and customs that regulated tin mining from early medieval times. For some these institutions carry the essence of a special constitutional status for Cornwall. Revivalists turned thankfully to 'Duchy' as a term for their land that avoided the distasteful description of 'county', but did not go the whole hog to 'nation'. Some enthusiastic Cornish nationalists go further. For them the relative autonomy and ambiguous rights and privileges of unrepealed charters and long-ignored liberties offer a way out of Cornwall's dilemma, stuck at the toe of an unsympathetic England.

So much so that the Stannary Parliament was unilaterally reconstituted in 1974. It remains to be seen how exactly these old feudal sovereignties can be sufficiently democratized to meet the needs of that modern and progressive European region that Cornwall could aspire to become given half the chance.

However, while different in many respects, Cornwall also shares familiar landscapes of power with other parts of Britain. The Normans built their castles in Cornwall; the church was until the sixteenth century, universal, or at least European; the gentry landscaped their estates and built their country houses in styles reminiscent of their class elsewhere. Castles, churches, country houses can still be 'Cornish' but in the sense of being located in Cornwall rather than sharing in the indefinable spirit of Cornishness.

Perran Round

The circular enclosure of Perran Round in the countryside between Perranporth and Goonhavern is the finest example of a medieval Plain-an-Gwarry in Cornwall. The name appears across west and mid-Cornwall: *plain-an-gwarry* is Cornish for 'playing place'. It was a place for performing religious plays which taught the Biblical stories to a largely illiterate population.

Religious plays, first mystery cycles and then more localized saints' plays, reflected a change in church policy in the thirteenth century and a desire to speak to the people

The saint's play was often performed on the saint's feast day.

The religious dramas of the period between the 1300s and the 1510s make up the bulk of the extant literature in Cornish. Unfortunately, unlike Welsh or Irish, there is no parallel secular literature or poetry, and virtually nothing in prose until the middle of the sixteenth century – a slight problem for those who would wish to revive 'authentic' medieval Cornish.

From the mention of local place-names, it's generally assumed that the plays, certainly the later ones, were penned at Glasney College, a religious house of canons situated in the valley below Penryn. This College (and the earlier town of Penryn) had been established by the Bishop of Exeter in the 1260s to increase his power and income in the west. Nonetheless, before the Reformation, it facilitated the emergence of a Cornish literary tradition and generated the raw material for the later revival of Cornish in the twentieth century. However, it meant the language was dangerously over-dependent on religious topics and church policies, and suffered badly when that religious policy changed after the 1530s.

in their own language. In most of Cornwall this meant in Cornish, and the plays were written and performed in Cornish. The mystery cycles were usually performed on three consecutive days every few years. These occasions were a mixture of holiday, entertainment and get-together – a kind of fourteenth-century Glastonbury festival.

Keigwin's Manor House

The sixteenth-century manor house, later divided into two separate buildings, standing in the middle of the village of Mousehole – Porthennis in Cornish – was the home of the Keigwin family. It survived the Spanish who, in 1595, raided and torched much of Mousehole and the parish church up the steep hill in Paul village.

Nowadays, Mousehole fits the bill as a stereotypical Cornish fishing village, its tiny cottages (a high proportion of which are now holiday and second homes) crowding the narrow streets surrounding a harbour and pier that date from the fourteenth century. It's best known for the story of *The Mousehole Cat* and, tragically, for the disastrous storm of 19 December 1981 when the local Penlee lifeboat, *Solomon Browne*, was lost and all her crew perished.

Yet for the Cornish it's also the place where Tom Bawcock's Eve takes place every Christmastime, as the dispossessed reclaim their village. And it has a special place in the history of the Cornish language, having a strong claim to be the last place where this distinctive Celtic language was spoken. Less than a stone's throw from Keigwin's manor house is the site of the cottage – now no more – that was home to Dolly Pentreath. Dolly won an ill-deserved fame as the 'last' Cornish speaker when she swore at a visiting gentleman in the 1760s. This was undeserved, as a year before she died a Mousehole fisherman – William Bodinar – wrote the last words in the historic Cornish language in a letter of 1776.

In the seventeenth century the Keigwins were part of a network that tried in vain to keep the Cornish language alive. They were prodded into action by William Scawen, a Cornishman far away in east Cornwall who in many ways was the first Cornish revivalist. In the later seventeenth century the baton was picked up by the Bosons of nearby Newlyn, among others, but these local enthusiasts failed to prevent the language's expiry.

Greystone Bridge

Greystone Bridge is one of four late medieval bridges spanning the Tamar downstream from the old Cornish capital of Launceston. The bridge was built around 1439 and carried (and still carries) the main road from Tavistock in Devon across the river into Cornwall.

Greystone is not quite as old as Horsebridge, built in 1437 a few miles to the south. Horsebridge was the lowest crossing of the Tamar for a couple of generations before Newbridge was constructed further down river near Gunnislake. This dates from around 1510, and was new only in relation to its more northerly predecessors. In 1644 it was the scene of a sharp skirmish between the Parliamentarian army of Lord Essex and Richard Grenville's Cornish Royalists, who were trying to bar the Parliamentarian force from Cornwall. Superior numbers won the day for the Parliamentarians, but victory was short-lived as they met their doom at the hands of King Charles and his army later in the year beside the River Fowey near Lostwithiel.

Neither was Greystone as old as Polson Bridge down the hill from Launceston. For centuries the main route into Cornwall, this bridge is now relatively peaceful, replaced by a sweeping dual carriageway to the south. Once its medieval arches signalled to the traveller an unmistakable transition, which is why bridges were so often accompanied by small chapels or religious statues. Now the consumer-citizens put their faith in sat-nav rather than saints as they hurtle across the ancient boundary, barely aware they are crossing a body of water. In the corner of their vision a 'Welcome to Kernow' sign flashes past, indicating some cultural passage that vaguely niggles the edge of their souls.

Men Scryfa

The moors of West Penwith sloping south-wards towards Mount's Bay have more than their fair share of archaeological treasures. In the modern period, this fragile moorland and its prehistoric remains have been threatened first by the mining industry, then by industrial-ized farming methods, and finally by the pres-sures of tourism and, according to some, by unsympathetic environmental 'management'.

Within a small area are Neolithic stone circles, Bronze Age round houses and field systems, Iron Age forts, settlements – includ-ing the second-century village at Chysauster – and standing stones from various eras.

A short walk across a now largely desert-ed landscape, passing several derelict nine-teenth-century farm buildings and cottages, brings us to the Men Scryfa. Standing in the middle of a field, this might be mistaken for a scratching post put up by a farmer for the relief of his cattle. But on it we can just make out the words *Rialobrani Cunovali fili* – 'Rialo-branus (or royal raven), son of Cunavolus'. *Men scryfa* in Cornish means 'writing stone', and the Latin script dates from somewhere between the fifth and seventh centuries, writ-ten on what is a Bronze Age standing stone.

The Men Scryfa (above). Men-an-Tol (facing page)

Rialobranus was being commemorated at a period when the Romans had left these shores to the tender mercies of the English, who were fortunately still confined to the eastern side of Britain. Rialobranus could have been a Cornish petty king or a tribal leader, and the stone might mark the boundary of his family's land. Legend places his castle at Lescudjack, yet the more obvious site would seem to be Chûn Castle, on the next hilltop about a mile to the west.

Just across the path from the Men Scryfa is the Men-an-Tol (or holed stone). This is a Bronze Age monument with an unclear purpose. The folk who set it up lived around here perhaps 1,500 or 2,000 years before those who carved the words on the Men Scryfa.

King Doniert's Stone

On a hillside on the edge of Bodmin Moor, looking south across the countryside around Liskeard, are two inscribed stones. These were arranged as we now see them in 1849, a broken cross-base next to a shaft. On the base are written the words *Doniert rogavit pro anima* – 'Doniert asks for prayers for his soul' – and the shaft is adorned with late ninth-century carvings. Could this be the same person as Dungarth, noted in Welsh histories, drowned in Cornwall around 875, and the last solid evidence for a Cornish king?

If so – and the stones are conveniently close to the fast-flowing River Fowey in the valley below – then it indicates that the battle of Hingston Down, fought near Callington around 838, was not the swansong of Cornish royalty. In the 830s a Cornish force allied itself with Danes returning from pillaging Brittany and together they attacked, or were attacked by, an army from Wessex. The Cornish and their allies were defeated, and presumably thereafter Cornish rulers paid homage to Wessex, the most powerful of the English kingdoms.

But defeat clearly did not mean assimilation. Cornish kings such as Doniert survived the wreckage of an independent Cornish kingdom, and Cornwall's Celtic culture was left relatively unscathed. More than a century after Doniert's death, Cornish was still spoken right up to the River Tamar. Cornwall was recognized as the homeland of the Cornish by the powerful King Athelstan in a treaty of the 930s. Although English administration very gradually infiltrated Cornwall, sometimes adopting and adapting older Celtic institutions such as the Hundreds, it took many centuries for Cornwall to be incorporated into its precocious and aggressive neighbour. Indeed, many would argue that this process was never completed.

Coinage

In 1198 the Stannary regulation of tin mining in Cornwall was reorganized by William de Wrotham. Cornish tin was already liable to taxation, incidentally at a higher rate than was tin from Devon – a reflection of Cornwall's subservient position. But de Wrotham rationalized its collection, ensuring that smelted tin blocks were brought at regular intervals to coinage towns to be assayed and given the official stamp of approval before onward sale.

This enabled coinage duties to be exacted, providing a most lucrative income for the Duchy of Cornwall after its inception in 1337. In return for supporting the Duke's lifestyle the Stannaries were regularly granted royal charters recognizing some of the miners' age-old customary rights. This was a medieval version of a protection racket. Miners were exempted from certain feudal services and allowed their own courts, and – in 1508 – were even given a measure of self-government. In return they were protected by the Crown as long as they paid their dues.

On such a basis rested the uneasy late-medieval compact between the Crown and Cornwall, the former guaranteeing the independence of the Cornish tinners, the latter supplying a steady flow of cash for Duchy and Crown coffers, and helping to keep the royal finances afloat.

At the coinages a corner of each block was cut and tested for purity; hence the word 'coinage' from the French for corner – *coin*

This nineteenth-century building in Truro stands on the site of the former coinage hall

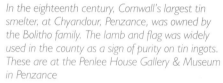

In the eighteenth century, Cornwall's largest tin smelter, at Chyandour, Penzance, was owned by the Bolitho family. The lamb and flag was widely used in the county as a sign of purity on tin ingots. These are at the Penlee House Gallery & Museum in Penzance

— rather than anything to do with money or taxation. Although Bodmin was an early coinage town it gave way to the main four coinage towns of Liskeard, Lostwithiel, Truro and Helston after the Black Death of 1349. Later, in 1663, Penzance was added as tin mining shifted westwards.

Coinage took place in coinage halls and the name Coinagehall Street in Helston reminds us of the former presence of a coinage hall there. In Truro a coinage hall stood at the east end of Boscawen Street, and was one of the principal buildings of the town. It dated from the 1300s and was used right up to the early 1830s. However, both the Helston and Truro coinage halls were demolished within a decade of the abolition of coinage dues in 1838.

Prayer Book
Rebellion

HEMM A GOVHA AN KOLL A
GOLLJI GLASNEDH HA'N
MERNANS A VILYOW A
WLASKARORYON GERNEWEK YN UNN
DHEFENDYA A GA FYDH, YETH
HA DEVOSOW KELTEK

THIS COMMEMORATES
THE LOSS OF GLASNEY COLLEGE
AND THE DEATH OF
THOUSANDS OF CORNISH PATRIOTS
IN DEFENCE OF THEIR FAITH, LANGUAGE
AND CELTIC CUSTOMS.

1549 - 1999
KERNOW ARTA

1549 Memorial

In contrast to the 1497 rising (see page 92 below), the far bloodier events of 1549 remained unmemorialized until a stone was raised at the lower end of Penryn in 1999. In 1549 a major rising took place in Cornwall, supported by a parallel rising at Sampford Courtenay in Devon. This was triggered by the imposition of the new English Prayer Book, seen by many as the final straw in a series of attacks by the newly Protestant church leaders on the traditional religious customs of the countryside.

While the majority of the demands that were made in 1549 were religious in tone and sought an end to the reforms, some were aimed at the gentry, widely condemned for supporting the changes. But in recent times more attention has been devoted to one of the dozen or more points made by the insurgents: that many Cornish did not understand the English of the new Prayer Book.

Traditionally known as the Prayer Book Rebellion, revisionist Cornish historians have re-termed it the Prayer Book War, preferring to view it as a national struggle against English oppression. Others have argued that the battlefield deaths and later executions of insurgents, who unsuccessfully laid siege to Exeter, directly extinguished the Cornish language and Celtic customs. In this way 1549 is seen as the dramatic turning point in Cornwall's past, triggering the end of constitutional autonomy and the destruction of its Celtic culture.

The traumatic events of this 'commotion time' were still fresh in the memory of the Cornish a generation or so later. John Norden noted in the 1580s that the Cornish harboured 'a kind of concealed envy against the English, whom they affect with a desire of revenge for their fathers' sake'. This memory had faded by the eighteenth century, but since the end of the twentieth century 1549 has been re-presented as part of a narrative that positions the Cornish as long-term victims of English oppression. This interpretation has gained ground, and in 2007 the then Bishop of Truro felt it necessary to apologize for the role of the Church of England almost 500 years before.

Restormel Castle

At the beginning of the twelfth century the most powerful Anglo-Norman family lording it over the Cornish peasantry was the Cardinhams. Their castle at Old Cardinham was the most westerly outpost (at the time) of this ruling elite. Sometime around 1100 the Cardinhams built another keep at Restormel, just up the valley from the new borough of Lostwithiel. However, a century later, in the early 1260s, this castle was wrenched out of their hands by Richard, Earl of Cornwall. It appears that Richard was not keen on potential rivals.

Richard's successor, Edmund, made Lostwithiel the centre of his administration and added to the castle, which remains the best example in Cornwall of a medieval castle. Yet all may not be quite as it appears. It has been suggested that this was not the ideal site for a military structure. The high ground to the south would have been preferable as it provided a viewpoint downriver towards the estuary. Instead, what could be seen from Restormel was virtually all of the medieval deer park stretching beyond its battlements. So perhaps Restormel was a sort of up-market hunting lodge, strategically placed not to command this important communications route, but as a viewing platform for the Cardinhams' hunts.

Indeed, it saw no recorded military action until 1644, when it was captured and temporarily garrisoned by Essex's doomed Parliamentarian army, before being recaptured by the Royalists.

Launceston Castle

Was Launceston Castle designed so that the natives would gaze upon it from a distance and shudder at the power of those who had built it? There was a wooden castle at Launceston at the time of Domesday Book in 1080, built by Robert, Count of Mortain, the Conqueror's half-brother and his main man in Cornwall. Perched on its commanding hill, it was no doubt hoped that it would deter a repeat of the events of 1069, when the Cornish had risen in rebellion and marched through Launceston to lay siege to Exeter.

The wooden structure had been replaced by stonework by the early 1200s, when it became the chief castle of Richard, Earl of Cornwall. In his time a new assize hall and other buildings were built in the castle bailey. The Normans had founded a string of castles from Kilkhampton in the north to Trematon in the south. These announced their control over Cornwall, but their location so far east

The Church of St Mary Magdalene (above). Launceston Castle and Southgate (facing page)

was also a sign of their hesitant and tentative grip on their newly conquered land.

Launceston became their main centre. By Richard's time it was the undisputed capital, its castle a slightly alien presence. Like London it lay on the very edge of the territory it administered. The castle shifted the focus from the older settlement of St Stephen across the Kensey valley to the north, to the newer settlement that grew up in the shelter of its keep. Launceston was the only town in Cornwall to have a town wall, the south gate of which is still a striking presence, while the other gates remain in street names. In the centre of the town we find the Church of St Mary Magdalene, rebuilt from 1511 to 1524 and decorated with superb carvings, all the more impressive for being carved in the unyielding native granite.

St Michael's Mount

St Michael's Mount, at Marazion, tops any league table of the most photographed Cor-
nish places. Its name suggests a religious connection, which dates from at least 1044, when a Benedictine priory was established here, a cell of the Norman Mont St Michel. It became Cornwall's major pilgrimage site in

Its Cornish name, which presumably predates the eleventh century, was the more prosaic · Carreg Looz en Cooz, or 'grey rock in the wood' – a reference to a time around 3,000 years ago when the Mount was still joined to the mainland and surrounded by a wood. In the 1400s the priory was suppressed as an alien institution, and the Mount's significance then became more military than religious. Supporters of the Lancastrians seized the Mount in 1473, and held out against a four-month siege. In 1497 one of the first actions of the pretender Perkin Warbeck, who had landed at Sennen, was to take the Mount.

With the suppression of the monasteries, the Mount passed to the Crown who then sold it on. In the early 1600s it was owned by the Bassets of Tehidy, but by the 1650s was in the hands of the St Aubyns of Clowance, who continued as its owners until the Mount was given over to the care of the National Trust in 1954.

Cut off from the mainland twice a day by the tide, the Mount retains an air of simple seclusion, and has managed to avoid the worst effects of commercialization that are all too evident at its big brother across the Channel in Normandy.

the medieval period, and has always enjoyed legendary status, whether as the site of the fabled Ictis, whence Phoenicians shipped Cornish tin, or as the home of a giant who amused himself by chucking rocks at other giants.

Roche Rock

The Celtic church in Cornwall is popularly supposed to have spawned many isolated hermitages and dispersed small monastic settlements, in contrast to the more hierarchical and disciplined English church. This distinction has, needless to say, been exaggerated, partly as a result of the later nineteenth-century fashion to draw sharply defined borders between 'Celts' and 'Saxons', and partly because of a later twentieth-century tendency to view the Celts as spiritual hippies, keen to commune with nature.

But suspend boring notions of historical 'truth' for a moment. The hermitage perched on Roche Rock is surely a classic statement of this traditional Celtic church, with its lonely single monk shunning society. John Norden, who visited Cornwall some time before 1584, clearly thought so. He described it as a 'very high, steep and craggy rock, upon the top whereof is placed a cell or hermitage, the walls whereof are partly wrought, and that with great labour, out of the obdurate rock: it stands upon the wild moors, far from common society, fittest for such votaries.'

In fact, the medieval hermitage and chapel, carved out of granite, only dated back to 1409. By the time Norden set eyes on it, it may have been remote and unvisited. But before the Protestant Reformation Roche Rock was a place of pilgrimage, maybe because of its impressive location. The chapel was probably built in recognition of this pre-existing role. To that extent there may well, in the 1400s, have been a constant stream of visitors to the place, and rather than a hairy hermit we should imagine a canny clergyman flogging indulgences to the visitors.

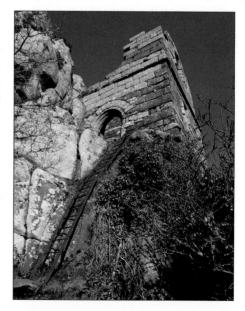

St Neot Church Windows

In the last years of the Catholic Church's primacy in England there was a boom in church building and restoration. Cornwall too had its share of church rebuilding, beginning in the 1400s. Bodmin, the largest church, was rebuilt between 1469 and 1491. St Mary Magdalene at Launceston is another major example, rebuilt between 1511 and 1524. This rash of investment in churches, reflecting the economic recovery of the fifteenth century, was cut short by the Reformation of the 1530s and '40s. It was not to be repeated on such a scale until the Victorian age.

Investment in the local parish fabric was not confined to the larger towns. In the village of St Neot, snug in its valley sheltered from the north and west by the moors, the church was rebuilt in the 1420s. Later, in the early 1500s, stained glass windows were put into the aisles, paid for by prominent local families and local guilds or groups. The windows tell the stories of Noah, the creation and the fall from paradise as well as recounting the more local legend of St Neot.

What makes St Neot unusual is the survival of its windows. In Protestant and Puritan thinking stained glass windows, ornate statues and decorative commemorations of local saints were a mere distraction from the Word of God, as written in the Holy Bible. The best context for spirituality was a simple one, freed from the superstitious mumbo-jumbo of a previous age. Crosses were beheaded, statues destroyed and windows smashed, especially in the mid-seventeenth century when religious anxieties were at their height. But St Neot's windows were hidden under whitewash until the storm had passed, and underwent a major restoration in the calmer 1820s.

Truro Cathedral

The towers of Truro Cathedral rear over the houses of the 'city' centre. This Early English-style cathedral with its gothic spires is in fact one of Cornwall's newer religious buildings. Its foundation stone was laid with much pomp and ceremony as late as 1880. The nave and the central tower were completed in 1898 and 1903 respectively, and the West Tower was finally finished in 1910.

In the generation-long building work the cathedral, as well as consuming several houses, incorporated the sixteenth-century north aisle of the former St Mary's parish church into its fabric. Its construction was the culmination of a thirty-year campaign to restore a Cornish diocese. The original diocese had been united with Crediton (later Exeter) in 1027, and for the best part of a millennium Cornwall's religious life was governed from Exeter.

But in the 1840s a High Church movement, harking back to the rituals and displays of the pre-Reformation church, gave Anglicanism renewed vigour. The nineteenth-century campaign for a Cornish see came about from a combination of two pressures. The first was the counter-offensive of the Church of England in Cornwall against a dominating Methodist nonconformity. At the 1851 religious census over two-thirds of Cornish people attended various Methodist chapels and only one-third the Anglican churches. The local parish church in Cornwall was by this time often an empty shell, largely ignored by its parishioners and frequented just for weddings, christenings, burials and on special occasions. Once chapels gained the right to carry out these functions even such vital events failed to fill the pews.

The second influence on the campaign for a diocese was a growing sense that Cornwall was different from Devon and deserved its own institutions. For this reason the campaign for a cathedral won some support even from Cornish nonconformists (although most remained lukewarm). The new Cornish diocese, when eventually granted, was and still is a hotbed of high-church Anglicanism, in a reaction against the formerly all-conquering Methodism.

Godolphin House

The Godolphins were typical of many Cornish landed gentry. The family was an old one, rooted in a spot west of Tregonning Hill in the parish of Breage. Fortune had smiled on them, for under their land lurked rich tin reserves. As mineral lords they were due a proportion of the tin raised, whether or not the miners made profits. On this basis the Godolphins grew rich, and built a new house in the late 1400s to replace the former castle, which became the site of formal gardens.

© NTPL/Aerial-Cam/Adam Stanford

their sails to the new Protestantism, could not prevent the Prayer Book Rising in 1549.

The house dates mainly from the seventeenth century, during the course of which Sidney Godolphin – poet and aesthete – gained posthumous fame after being shot in the service of the King in the civil wars at Chagford in Devon. He became a symbol of the Cornish landed class's devotion to the royal family.

Another Sidney, born in 1645, two years after the first Sidney was killed, became MP for nearby Helston, and a client of the up-and-coming Marlborough family. This Sidney, later Earl, served Queen Anne as Lord Treasurer from 1702 to 1710, and has a better claim than Robert Walpole to have been Britain's first Prime Minister. He steered the Act of Union with Scotland through Parliament in 1707, and financed the long war of the Spanish Succession against the French. The costs of this war eventually lost Godolphin his post and he was dismissed in 1710, to die at St Albans in Hertfordshire two years later.

In the eighteenth century the family declined and gradually ran out of male heirs, their estate passing to the absentee Duke of Leeds in 1785. The house was left virtually undisturbed for 200 years until the final decades of the 1900s.

The family gained political prominence to add to their economic security in the days of Henry VIII. Their rapid move to ensure law and order in 1537 and 1548 defused potentially serious risings by the common people. But even the Godolphins, adroitly trimming

Lanherne Manor House

Despite its proximity to the teeming honey-pots of Cornish tourism and an airport which we are sagely assured will be the unlikely driver of a Cornish economic miracle, the Vale of Mawgan is a quiet, out-of-the-way place. Next to the church is the old manor house of the Arundell family – Lanherne.

The Arundells had been at Lanherne from the thirteenth century, and rose to prominence during the rumbustious fifteenth century. In those times men returned from fighting in the long wars with the French, or from the interminable squabbles over the succession to the English throne, and had few skills other than soldiering. In Cornwall lawless times were given an extra twist by the constant struggle to control tin and its sources. But despite this, or perhaps because of it, the Arundells prospered.

However, in the 1530s and '40s, when most of the Cornish gentry kept their heads down and went along with the new-fangled religious reforms emanating from London, the Arundells clung to the old ways. The family became Cornwall's highest-profile recusants, refusing to give up their Catholicism. They were linked to Cuthbert Mayne, a Catholic priest executed at Launceston in 1577 who had ministered to the Arundells and other Catholic Cornish families.

Religious nonconformity in those times smacked of political subversion, and in the 1580s the head of the Arundell family was imprisoned in London for nine years at the Queen's pleasure. The last Arundell, Sir John, died in 1701. But by this time the family had fallen as quickly as it had risen. It is fitting that their house, an Elizabethan building dating from those troubled times in the later sixteenth century, became a Carmelite convent in 1794.

The grounds house a tenth-century cross, claimed to be the finest example of a decorated cross in Cornwall. But all is not what it seems. The cross was moved here from Roseworthy, many miles to the west near Camborne. At least one other cross was found decorated in a similar fashion even further west, at Sancreed.

Antony House

Antony House, overlooking the River Lynher, is significant for two reasons. First, it is the finest example of a classical country house in Cornwall, completed in 1721 of Pentewan stone. Second, this place was the seat of the Carew family from the later 1400s.

The most famous Carew was Richard, born in 1554. In his forties, Richard compiled the *Survey of Cornwall*, published in 1602. The Survey was one of the first antiquarian county histories to appear in the British Isles, and provides a beguiling picture of late-sixteenth-century Cornwall. It contains detailed descriptions of the Tudor mining industry, of farming practices, the state of Cornish towns and of pastimes such as hurling, among a multitude of other topics,

However, Carew lived near to the Cornish border and his writings sometimes betray a haziness about the society of the far west. Though a renowned linguist, author of translations from Spanish and Italian and reputedly fluent in five languages, these did not include Cornish. Carew's musings on a language still widely spoken in his time west of Truro are tantalizingly sketchy.

The Elizabethan Carew family was part of an emerging network of gentry power located in south-east Cornwall. In the seventeenth century this included the Grenvilles of Cotehele, the Eliots of St Germans and the newly wealthy Roberts (or Robartes) of Lanhydrock. These were more likely to be Puritans than their landed counterparts further west, and provided a core of support for Parliament in the civil wars.

The Carew family in the seventeenth and eighteenth centuries reflected the wider loyalties of Cornish gentry politics. In the 1640s it furnished both Parliamentarians and Royalists, and in 1715 Sir William Carew, who built the present house, was arrested as a suspected Jacobite sympathizer. Such politics were typical of the early eighteenth-century Cornish gentleman.

Boconnoc

From Richard Carew in the late 1500s to Richard Polwhele in the early 1800s, Cornish writers were prone to claim that all Cornish gentry were 'cousins', rooted in the land and with lineages stretching back deep into its immemorial past. Given the constant replenishment of this class by new money, both Cornish and non-Cornish, such a claim to pedigree was always overplayed.

Boconnoc, near Lostwithiel, is a prominent example, its purchasers providing a link to late eighteenth-century British parliamentary politics. In the 1710s Thomas Pitt, former Governor of Fort St George in Madras, India, bought the Boconnoc estate. Pitt was the grandfather of William Pitt the elder and great-grandfather of the younger Pitt, two Prime Ministers who towered over British politics.

Thomas Pitt began the present house, replacing a medieval building. His son, like all the first-born male Pitts also confusingly called Thomas, was Lord Warden of the Stannaries and Steward of the Duchy of Cornwall. However, the unexpected death of the Duke of Cornwall in 1751 pitched Thomas into serious financial difficulties, and he had to leave Boconnoc in 1755, six years before his death.

Boconnoc and its park were left to slowly decay until his son came into his inheritance and restored the house after 1762. It is likely that this Thomas, the first Lord of Camelford, also completed the landscaped park in the 500-year-old deer park, and built the obelisk there in 1771. After the Pitt line ended in 1804, the Fortescue family later added the formal terraces and gardens.

The Pitts, with their social and economic networks centred on London and the governing elite, were relatively marginal figures in

eighteenth-century Cornish society. In many ways they treated Cornwall as a refuge from the hurly-burly of government and court life, early forerunners of a tendency that had become increasingly and depressingly familiar by the late-twentieth century.

Caerhays Castle

Caerhays Castle, overlooking Porthluney Cove, near Gorran, was begun around 1808 for the Trevanions, an old Cornish family who had lived in the district since at least the early 1500s, when they supplied four sheriffs in the space of just 12 years. But the costs of con-structing this impressive house proved too much, and the Trevanions sold out to new money in the shape of Michael Williams, who bought Caerhays in 1854.

Michael Williams was only three generations descended from a working miner – John Williams – who had become manager of Poldice Mine in Gwennap and made his fortune out of the expanding copper mines of west Cornwall. By the 1820s the Williams' business partnership was operating across Britain, and had interests in copper smelting works in south Wales. Michael Williams became the Liberal MP for West Cornwall in the 1850s, and his son John Michael Williams, educated at Charterhouse School, was described on his death in 1880 as 'probably the most wealthy man in Cornwall'. The family had come a long way in just 150 years.

There is little direct evidence now at Caerhays of the mining and smelting wealth that lay behind the rise of the Williamses. Instead, the gardens are home to one of Britain's best collections, if not the best collection, of rhododendrons and magnolias – a striking sight in the late spring. The transformation of the family from canny mine investors and operators to leaders in the nursery business and garden tourism speaks volumes about a more general shift in Cornish fortunes.

Sacred Places

All peoples and nations have places they regard as significant. The English have Shakespeare's birthplace, the Scots the site of the battle of Bannockburn. Identities are etched into the landscape and inscribed on the map. Sometimes sacred places are literally sacred, imbued with religious significance as well as secular meaning. Sometimes places can be shared by two or more groups. An example of this is Gwennap Pit, special for many because it was the open-air cathedral of the Cornish, and central to the Methodism that dominated nineteenth- and early twentieth-century Cornish life. But it is also important for many Methodists beyond Cornwall

because of its role in the early history of that denomination.

In Cornwall it is not easy to identify unambiguously sacred places. In one sense all the places mentioned in this book are 'sacred' because they have a meaning or meanings for Cornish people. The degree of sacredness depends on our perspective on the past or where we hail from. The emotional resonance of Carn Brea or Kit Hill will vary depending on whether we were brought up in Camborne or Callington. For those brought up in Bude or St Just, they may have different meanings.

Natural features can be sacred places because of the way they evoke meaning. This meaning may be specific to us as individuals, inducing memories of childhood or of family now passed on. Or they may stand in for some larger entity, representing a complex whole in simple terms. Thus, the ruined engine house silhouetted on the cliffs screams 'Cornwall' to millions, and is an image that has resonance far beyond the Cornish themselves. Symbols such as cliffs and rolling surf are grist to the mill of the advertising

industry, investing commodities with the magic ingredient of 'Cornishness'. Ultimately there is something shallow about this, a limited repertoire of signs and images that spell 'Cornwall' in unmistakeable terms but with all the subtlety of a sledgehammer.

Special places for the Cornish are, in contrast, more intricate and complicated. They could well be a natural feature, a stretch of coastline, a patch of vegetation, the shape of a familiar horizon. But more often sacred places are shaped by the hand of man more than by nature, even if we suppose that 'nature' can ever exist independent of human impact. Fishing villages, individual buildings, archaeological or industrial remains, even whole towns can fulfil the role of sacred places for us.

Tintagel Castle

To many Cornish people 'English' Heritage's management of Tintagel Castle is a slap in the face. Well before the English ever set foot in these islands, Tintagel was a site of special significance. A series of Roman milestones pointed the way to this spot and hint at its importance in earlier times. Perhaps it was a centre for the collection of tribute or a place of particular religious significance.

Its promontory, jutting out into the Atlantic, commands a view of the north coast from the Camel estuary to Hartland Point, and this alone would have made it a lookout point for anyone watching the sea either for traders or raiders. The evidence points to the first of these. Tintagel is the site of the largest collection of fragments of sixth-century Mediterranean pottery anywhere in Britain. Exactly why ships should have made the difficult journey around Land's End to this spot remains a mystery, but presumably indicates its importance in post-Roman times.

Its place in Celtic society meant that it became one of the locations for stories and memories of King Arthur. These tales were exported to the Continent along with the Tristan and Isolde saga, and then re-imported in the twelfth century, repackaged in chivalric and knightly terms more suited to the later medieval period.

Tintagel's pull remained strong in the 1300s when Richard, Earl of Cornwall, built a castle there, the remains of which cling to the cliffs today. Richard was presumably making a statement about his power and trying to link it to folk memories of British kings and princes. His castle never had an obvious military function, and was derelict within a century and a half of its construction. Nonetheless, its presence and Tintagel's connections with the Arthurian legends many centuries later drew businessmen to build a hotel on the opposite headland in 1893, hoping to benefit from the newly opened North Cornwall railway.

Nowadays, thousands of tourists from all corners of Europe and further afield descend on the tourist village of Tintagel, known as Trevena until the late 1800s. Most of them are intent on negotiating the steep steps of the castle, hoping to gaze on the same landscape that the bewitching but infuriatingly intangible Arthur did a millennium and a half ago.

Dozmary Pool

Dozmary Pool lies in the heart of Bodmin Moor in a shallow valley over 270 metres above sea level. At first sight this small, uninspiring stretch of grey water, its surface ruffled by never-ending wind and broken by almost constant rain, may seem less than extraordinary. Nowadays, it's dwarfed by the vast Colliford Reservoir across the hill to the west. Yet it has been described as being as sacred to the Cornish as the Ganges is to the Hindus.

Most visitors would wonder why. Arriving there in cars loaded with computerized gadgetry and safely alienated from the world outside, they are likely to gaze upon the pool uncomprehendingly, shrugging their shoulders after a few minutes before moving on impatiently to the next tourist attraction.

However, show some imagination and consider people in former times who had made a long and wearisome journey to this lonely spot. Listen to the song of the skylarks and the unending noise of the wind, now hissing, now howling, while the reeds rustle at the edge of the pool. Look at the enigmatic water, shifting from grey to blue as the showers pass overhead. Can you see how the pool could well take on a different meaning?

At a time when we were not so far down the road to destroying the natural world, we may have been keener to believe that this really was the place where King Arthur's great sword Excalibur was thrown by Sir Bedivere, only to be caught by an arm 'clad in white', rising out of the waters. Or we may have found the story of Tregeagle a very

credible one. Tregeagle was a legendary figure based on a real and clearly unpopular steward employed by the Robartes family at Lanhydrock in the seventeenth century. After his death Tregeagle's soul was summoned to be judged for his oppressive behaviour while alive, and he was doomed to the eternal punishment of emptying Dozmary Pool with a limpet shell. To make the task less easy the shell had a hole bored in it. Tregeagle eventually departed westwards, chased away by a crowd of angry and shrieking demons during a raging gale. He resumed his punishment at Roche Rock, this time plaiting ropes of sand, a task made even more hopeless by the distance of Roche from the nearest beach.

Angove's Statue

In 1966, Mebyon Kernow, then a nationalist pressure group, set a memorial plaque in the church wall at St Keverne. This was a tribute to the events of almost 500 years before when Michael Joseph An Gove (the Smith) led the people of his village in a rising in 1497. As the insurgents trekked east they picked up support. Most notably, they were joined by Thomas Flamank, a Bodmin lawyer, who gave the rising its (now lost) rationale.

That it was caused by a great deal more than local annoyance over higher taxes is implied by the orderly and strategic route the protestors took as they struck across southern England, heading for the heart of English government in London. Panicked by the approaching host, Henry VII used the army he had raised to fight the Scots to confront his adversaries at Blackheath.

There the Cornish met their inevitable defeat. Outnumbered and, more crucially, outgunned, their leaders were captured. Michael Joseph's defiant words as he was taken to his execution – 'We shall have a name perpetual and a fame permanent and immortal' – were inscribed on the memorial plaque in 1966.

In 1997, on the five-hundredth anniversary of the event, the epic march across England from St Keverne to London was re-enacted. This attracted a lot of media and popular curiosity, and led to a growing interest in Cornwall's Tudor heritage of resistance and rebellion. One result was a rash of commodities cashing in on the interest, including Cornish Rebellion bottled beer. But more permanently a Trust raised the money to erect a statue to Angove and Flamank on the outskirts of St Keverne. This now stands as a reminder of the time when this small village on the remote Lizard peninsula shook the very foundations of the English state.

Wreath on the wall of St Keverne church

Piran's Oratory

Holidaymakers enjoying the 'miles of white sand' and the 'change of pace' promised at Perran Sands holiday park would no doubt be surprised to learn that they were staying within a mile of one of the sacred sites of Cornwall's religious history. This was Lanpiran, a monastic site that in the medieval period became a major place of pilgrimage. The church rebuilt on this site in the 1000s housed a shrine with the relics of St Piran and the teeth of St Brendan and St Martin, and before the sixteenth century people flocked here to see these marvels.

Today a stone cross and low walls announce the remains of the eleventh-century church, overwhelmed by that same white sand ceaselessly blown inland from the wide sweep of Perran sands by the prevailing westerlies. When it was originally built the church would have been situated among fields and downland. By the 1700s these had disappeared under a barren landscape of ever-shifting dunes. The church was closed and a new one opened a few miles inland in 1804 at a safe distance from the encroaching sand.

Lanpiran was not the first church in this parish but the second. A few hundred metres to the west is St Piran's oratory, a tiny church built perhaps in the seventh century. This was lost for hundreds of years, buried by the sand and only revealed in 1835. A protective cover was placed over it in the early 1900s, but it was reburied in 1981 to preserve it. It is now being revealed again, fittingly reappearing just as the Cornish gained offical recognition of their national minority status.

The oratory is dedicated to Piran, one of the Irish 'saints' who arrived in the fifth or sixth century. These saints had a fondness for unconventional modes of travel. Piran sailed on a millstone; one of his colleagues is alleged to have arrived on a leaf. However he arrived, the original Piran would no doubt be amused to see his modern status as Cornwall's patron saint. This stems from his role as the patron saint of tinners, and he now has his own flag and even had a beer named after him.

St Piran's Ale (above). Stone cross, church and formerly buried oratory site (facing page, left to right)

Royal Albert Bridge

The Cornish relationship with the bridges that carry the main railway line and the A38 over the Tamar is ambiguous to say the least. We use them unthinkingly for shopping trips to Plymouth or, if of a masochistic bent, to suffer the agonies of supporting Plymouth Argyle. We pass over them on our way to places further away, hastening on as quickly as possible through the English county of Devonshire. And yet, on returning over these bridges, we feel at home and the words of the Cornish national anthem 'Here's 20,000 Cornishmen shall know the reason why' may float unbidden into our thoughts.

The bridges symbolize Cornwall's relationship with England. They are unmistakeable evidence of our connections with our neighbours, routes for visitors and migrants alike to come to Cornwall. But they are also borders of our imagination. So steeped are we in the symbolism of crossing this border – one of the oldest political frontiers in Europe – that we rarely appreciate the functional structures that enable our crossing to take place.

Isambard Kingdom Brunel's railway bridge, it is fair to say, attracts more affection than the road bridge, opened in 1961 at just about

the same time that migration to Cornwall began to hit record levels. For many the road bridge is directly implicated in the process of uncontrollable and undirected change that

followed. The railway bridge was built much earlier, in 1857–9, and opened by Prince Albert, who gave his name to it. Towering over the older parts of Saltash it was a monument to Victorian modernity, replacing the ferry that had plied between Saltash and Devon since the thirteenth century, and uniting the West Cornwall Railway with the English network.

Bodmin Jail

Bodmin was Cornwall's principal town for about a thousand years. At the time of Domesday Book in 1080 it was the largest borough in Cornwall, and its numerous medieval religious foundations – a monastery (later a priory), friary, lazar houses and hospitals – suggest that it had been a centre for Cornish kings and bishops when Cornwall was an independent kingdom.

When the Normans arrived Launceston became their centre, and when they were confident enough to venture westwards, their administrative town of choice was nearby Lostwithiel. But Bodmin remained Cornwall's largest town. Its parish church, splendidly rebuilt in the fifteenth century, was the largest in Cornwall. Significantly, the town was also the focus for the proclamations and gatherings of those who resisted the Crown in 1483, 1497 and 1549.

By the 1800s Bodmin was sharing assize courts with Launceston, which was too far east to serve Cornwall's growing population. In 1836 Bodmin effectively became Cornwall's capital. It was already home to other buildings that hinted at this role, the most imposing being the County jail. This was built in 1779, using the labour of French prisoners of war. Rebuilt in 1855–8 with cells for 129 prisoners, it continued to act as Cornwall's prison until 1916. Part of it became a navy prison in the 1880s, and this continued until 1922, but the building finally ceased to be a jail in 1927 and gradually decayed until recently. Until 1862 public executions took place here – events which brought crowds of onlookers and much-needed trade to the town. The last execution took place at the Jail in 1902 behind closed doors, when a man from St Erth was hanged for murder.

Bodmin was also the location of Cornwall's Lunatic Asylum, begun in 1820 and added to at various points over the following 65 years. With both prison and asylum, Bodmin gained a rather forbidding reputation among generations of Cornish people, for whom being 'sent to Bodmin' served as a grisly warning of their fate if they didn't mend their ways.

The town declined relatively in the eighteenth and nineteenth centuries, as wealth and employment followed the mines westwards. In the 1870s, and again in 1889, it lost to Truro in the battle to site Cornwall's cathedral and County Council. Then it stagnated, with a loss of confidence. In the 1960s Bodmin was the only Cornish town to volunteer for 'overspill' population from London.

Duchy Palace

In most countries the sacred sites of their past are accorded due reverence, conserved, protected and interpreted so that the masses can have no doubt as to their significance. In modern times, such sites and buildings have taken on hugely enhanced importance for governments using nationalism to control and cajole their people.

The state of the former Duchy Palace at Lostwithiel therefore might be an indication of the invisibility of the Cornish nation. Despite a recent makeover and a new roof, the building still sadly lacks informative interpretation plaques. In its prime, it looked out over open ground to the river. But now it sits unostentatiously opposite some nondescript post-war housing. Even though little effort is made to tell the tale, passers-by may occasionally wonder what functions such a large barn ever served.

These are the cryptic material remains of the secretive government of the Duchy of Cornwall and the earlier earldom that over the centuries leached so much of the profits of Cornish tin. The complex of buildings on the large site now known as the Duchy Palace first appeared during the earldom of

Edmund in the 1280s. In fact it was never a palace. This place operated for four centuries as an administrative centre, offices for the man who managed the earl's and (after 1337) the duke's interests, a venue for county courts and the election of county Members of Parliament, a location for the Stannary prison and the site of a coinage hall and a later convocation hall, where meetings of the tinners' parliaments took place.

However, in 1644, in a symbolic act of destruction, Parliamentary troops gutted the main buildings. Thereafter, the Great Hall lay in ruins, its purposes and role in Cornish life largely unappreciated and unmourned.

Gwennap Pit

Gwennap Pit, tucked away in the quiet lanes between Redruth and the former mining villages of Carharrack and St Day, is a trim and neatly circular grassy amphitheatre. It wasn't always so. It took on its present form in 1807, when local Methodists reconstructed it as their own outdoor cathedral. Before then, the site was a chaotic cavity, a large disorderly pit squeezed between stony mine burrows and smoking engine houses, through which the lane from Redruth to Carharrack meandered.

However, this chasm provided a perfect location in which to address large crowds. And this is what John Wesley began to do in the later eighteenth century. Wesley made his first journey to Cornwall in 1743. He then visited Cornwall almost annually until his death in 1791, making his last visit to the Pit in 1789. His simple message of salvation through faith struck an immediate chord among a population seeking consolation in a world that was rapidly changing. The growth of copper mines, the prosperity of which flowed from anonymous and unpredictable price movements, added new uncertainties to the more familiar foes of weather and disease. People increasingly dependent on the mine for their wages sought spiritual solace in Wesley's preaching.

In England, Methodism grew slowly in the late eighteenth and early nineteenth centuries through the teaching of devoted con-

verts to small groups in barns and houses. In contrast, in Cornwall Methodism grew in sudden spurts of excitable revivalism. These usually involved emotional outdoor mass meetings, accompanied by histrionic moan-ings and hot fanaticism. Gwennap Pit, now so calm and orderly, is in fact a monument to that earthier, more basic, more public and primitive Methodism in Cornwall – appealing to passion as much as reason.

Carn Brea

Carn Brea, with its monument, is the unmistakeable symbol of home for those who hail from the parishes of Redruth, Camborne and Illogan that sprawl around the north of this hill. The monument to Francis Basset of nearby Tehidy was put up in 1836. The Bassets – an old Cornish family – made their fortune from the expansion of copper and tin mining in this district. Francis, ennobled fancifully as Lord de Dunstanville, was a reactionary and fiery conservative. In 1801 he hastened back to Cornwall to ensure that some hungry food rioters were properly hanged and not, as was usual, let off with transportation.

The Bassets had been major boroughmongers in the 1700s, making money from the proliferation of parliamentary seats in

Cornwall. They were not exactly keen on the growing reform movements of the 1800s. In the 1880s, Francis' descendant, Arthur, aroused the ire of the radicals of Camborne-Redruth by demanding a large increase in royalties from Dolcoath mine at a time of economic difficulties, as well as attempting (unsuccessfully) to block footpaths along the north coast.

The family had built a hunting lodge on Carn Brea before 1500, this now being Cornwall's most dramatically located restaurant. Today the Carn houses fewer people than it did two millennia ago when the hut circles that can still be seen on the summit were occupied. This Iron Age hill fort – the largest in Cornwall – was itself sited within the ramparts of a much older, Neolithic fort. Hundreds of arrowheads discovered here suggest it was a place of conflict somewhere around 5,000 years ago.

Conflicts around the Carn continue to this day. In the 1800s the land to north and south became Cornwall's most industrialized landscape, littered with mine burrows, punctuated by the chimneys of engine houses, pockmarked by shafts. In the twentieth century this mining landscape was cleared to the north, replaced by faceless factories and industrial estates. In the twenty-first century

a 'Heartlands' project appeared here, with café, shops, a children's play area, 'diaspora gardens' and restored mine surface buildings. This was designed to help attract new residents to the 4,500 more houses planned for the district. Meanwhile Carn Brea itself laconically watches the changing scene at its feet.

Groups

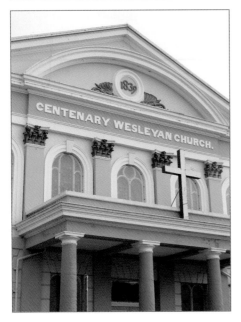

Methodism: churches at Camborne (left) and Chacewater (above). Supporting Cornwall at Twickenham, 1999 (facing page)

There is a powerful myth that the Cornish were by nature great individualists. Put positively, they refused to be constrained by fashion or custom and struck out on their own. They were hardy emigrants on the frontiers of empire, religious nonconformists and free-thinkers or self-reliant men economically, free from the 'tyranny' of either trade unions or giant corporations. Put negatively, they could never agree on anything and were fundamentally incapable of organizing themselves. They constantly squabbled over minor and unimportant issues, whether where to build railway lines (in the 1800s), or how to spell revived Cornish (a century later).

This myth was fostered mainly in the early twentieth century as the Cornish clung on

to a doomed Liberal Party that, stripped of its radicalism, became lifeless and inert. In similar fashion the once-dynamic Methodism now basked in former glories, and seemed incapable of responding to the temptations of modernity.

Historians today are belatedly chipping away at this myth of the Cornish individualist. The myth is reinforced by ideas of the romantic Celt, heroically tilling his rough patch of moorland, living with his family in an isolated farmstead while nearby early Christian monks shunned society in their comfortless hermitages. It is now suggested that Cornish peasant farmers actually shared strips in open fields from the seventh to the sixteenth centuries. This was a communal and co-operative existence. Farmers came together regularly to reallocate their strips of land in conditions of rough equality. In religion too, the idea of the romantic Celtic church is being seriously questioned.

Even in the nineteenth century there was more evidence of co-operation than of indi-

Padstow Obby Oss (above). Helston Furry Dance and Penzance's Golowan (facing page)

vidualism. Miners and fishermen worked in small groups, often linked by kinship. In the wider community, a 'spirit of aggregation' was noted in 1857, which 'finds a vent in camp-meetings, temperance parties and monster tea drinkings'. Earlier, in the 1820s, Cornish historian Samuel Drew wrote that the Cornish were 'accustomed to associate in bodies,

they mutually encourage each other to per-severance, even on occasions when all rational hopes of success have taken their leave.'

This predilection to associate in groups continued into the twentieth century. From 1908 onwards the Cornish (at first just men, later men and women) were more likely to congregate to support their rugby

team than their chapels. People flocked to watch their heroes at times when the team was doing well. In 1908, 1928, 1968, 1969 and 1989–91 Cornwall was awash with patriotic fervour. At such times Wilkie Collins' words of 1850 – 'a man speaks of himself as Cornish in much the same way as a Welshman speaks of himself as Welsh' – seemed to ring true.

At a more local level, a vigorous tradition of community feasts and festivals has been resurrected over the past decade or two. Old festivals such as Padstow Obby Oss or the Helston Furry Dance continue to attract thousands, while new arrivals such as Camborne's Trevithick Day, Redruth's Murdoch Day or Penzance's Golowan have become established on the annual social calendar.

Billy Bray's Chapel

Methodism prospered because, as an organization, it was flexible and able to cope with a rapidly changing and industrializing society more easily than an Anglican establishment shackled to its medieval parishes. It was also able to speak to the people in their own accent. It did this through co-opting the enthusiasm and energy of a host of lay preachers, local men and originally some women who supplemented the itinerant preachers sent out to minister to local circuits. The role of lay preachers, who combined preaching with a full-time job, was

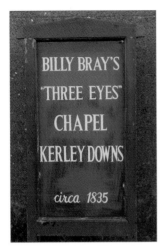

particularly important in the small country chapels that materialized after 1760.

Born in 1794, Billy Bray was a miner who first appeared on the Bible Christian circuit as a local preacher in 1824. Bray was a child at the time of the great 1799 revival which swept across Cornwall and drew many into Methodist membership. He was a young man when the next great 'awakening' in 1814 caused a whirlwind of religious fervour to sweep across Cornwall.

After these great years of Methodism, during which it grew from a sect to the dominant denomination of Cornwall, it split into rival factions. The Bible Christians were one of these, working in the more rural areas less touched by earlier Methodist activity. They appealed to the poor and dispossessed, and held firm to the emotional revivalism that characterized Cornish Methodism.

Bray became an icon of this simple but fiery evangelical creed. He was involved in the building of at least three chapels near to his birthplace at Twelveheads, on the edge of the mining district, of which only the one at Kerley Downs remains. He died in 1868 at the good age of 74, and was buried in Baldhu churchyard, ironically next to a new church built by the Anglicans in a belated attempt to counter the attraction of Methodism.

Huer's Hut

Newquay is often in the news for its rowdy late-night boozing. Cornwall's answer to Blackpool is a crowded place in summer, its population temporarily swollen as it becomes for a few months by far the biggest town in Cornwall. These days, even in winter it's hardly quiet, its population having more than doubled since the 1950s, and attracting local youngsters to its lively pub and club scene.

Outside Cornwall Newquay is best known for its fine beaches and surfing culture. Inside, it's become less well known over the years, as locals often shun the tacky tourism that grips Newquay in its sickly embrace.

But Newquay had a life before the tourist hordes descended: it was not dissimilar to other Cornish coastal towns. Originally a small fishing village – its Cornish name Towan Blistra means 'dune by the harbour of boats' – there were grandiose plans to make it a major clay and ore port in the nineteenth century when the railway linked it to the industrial districts around St Austell. That was not to be, and Newquay found its destiny in the mass sun, sea and sand tourism that reached Cornwall in the 1950s.

Yet Newquay is not all luxury flats that serve as weekend boltholes for jaded and overpaid City bankers or upper-class surfing wannabes, nor is it all down-market, one-room apartments for the less well-off. Near the Atlantic Hotel, itself a classic monument to late nineteenth-century British tourism, we find the whitewashed huer's hut. This acts as a reminder of the days when shoals of pilchards would arrive annually off the coast. A huer would wait at the hut to spot their arrival. On his shout of 'Heva, heva' (Cornish for a swarm or shoal), local men set forth in their seine boats to harvest this manna.

Seining villages like Newquay became a hive of activity for a few short weeks as every spare hand was commandeered to man the boats, directed to the fish by the huer. Once landed, it was the turn of the women of the town to 'bulk' the pilchards – prepare them with salt ready to be pressed into barrels – before the fish was exported to the Mediterranean. Now the cry of the huers and the chat of the bulking women have disappeared, replaced by the raucous screech of over-fed gulls fighting to steal the visitors' fish and chips.

St Ives

In the nineteenth century St Ives was a town where the bulk of the people were dependent on two occupations. Upalong were mining families who worked in the nearby tin mines. Downalong were fishermen and their families. Serving these close-knit communities were the shopkeepers and craftsmen.

In the years from the 1870s to the 1920s the local mines closed down one by one. Simultaneously, the vitality of the fishing industry suffered as steam trawlers from up-country replaced sail. Fishermen found it harder to compete, and Cornish fleets were decimated, reaching their low point in the 1930s. Miners and fishermen alike were re-housed in the council estate up the hill. But by this time St Ives was rapidly gaining another source of income. The arrival of the railway had triggered the growth of tourism.

At first this was confined to the relatively wealthy, some of whom began to colonize the coast eastwards as housing spread along the road to Lelant and on the coast at Carbis Bay. Then in the 1950s mass tourism made its appearance, and the sea front at St Ives became a heaving mass of strangers every summer. The locals watched their town change in front of their eyes – with resignation, concern, or an eye for a quick profit. The recent history of this diverse and lively community is brilliantly reconstructed in the novels of local writer NR Phillips.

At the same time as artists began to settle in Newlyn they began painting in St Ives. But St Ives attracted a younger group with fresh ideas, and 'realism' was replaced by 'modernism'. The place became a mecca for artistic innovation in the middle of the twentieth century. Not all of this was imported; one of the most creative modernist painters was Peter Lanyon who, before his untimely death from a gliding accident, fused a deep respect for his native landscape with a modernist interpretation.

Nowadays St Ives is a centre of 'gourmet tourism'. It also hosts the Tate Gallery, the apex of a cultural tourism triangle whose other points are the Maritime Museum at Falmouth and The Eden Project. But the glossy veneer hides another story. In the heart of the old community, over a third of the houses are second homes and holiday lets, a figure exceeded only by Polzeath, resort of choice for public-school boys and girls.

St Ives harbour (top); Tate St Ives (bottom left); the Porthminster Café (bottom right)

How Others See Us

The moors of West Penwith... remote from the metropolis (above and facing page)

Cornwall is one of the most visited places in the UK. Every year four million or so join the half million plus who live here, squeezing into this narrow strip of land beyond the Tamar. At the same time, however, Cornwall must lay claim to be one of the least well under-stood places in the UK. This is because of the power of some underlying stereotypes.

A simplistic equation of distance from the observer with distance from 'civilization' can be noted from at least the sixteenth cen-tury and probably a lot earlier. The largest number of people tended to live in capital cities. As these were the places where gov-ernment, power and influence resided, then their assumption that the metropolis was the epitome of civilization tended to dominate. From that perspective, the further people lived from the metropolis then the less civi-lized they were.

Before the 1800s this gave rise to the idea of Cornwall being 'West Barbary', fascinating but preferably to be avoided. Ideas about the wild Cornish savage were transformed dur-ing the nineteenth century into a picture of a domesticated savage (as opposed to the Irish

who remained much less cuddly). By the late 1800s Cornwall was still being viewed as the opposite to sophisticated urban living – its people closer to nature and living simpler traditional lives – but this had now become appealing and attractive, as disillusion with urban values grew.

From this stems the modern perception of Cornwall as being somehow faintly green, a perfect place in fact for The Eden Project, wind turbines and 'lifestyle'. This stereotype then helps produce, but at the same time shrouds, a reality which includes a popula-

tion rise of 50 per cent in just 50 years, and higher levels of house-building than virtually anywhere else in Britain. The problems caused by such a rate of growth then become a taboo subject. This is partly because discussing them challenges those interests that profit from selling Cornwall. And partly because they confront simple metropolitan stereotypes of Cornwall as a 'deeply rural' place with a 'slower pace of life'. (Actually, rural population densities are higher in mid and west Cornwall than in most rural parts of southern England.)

Watergate Bay (top), home to Fifteen Cornwall restaurant (above). Falmouth Oyster Festival (facing page) is an annual event

As well as being one of the most visited places, Cornwall has been one of the most written about. Today books are churned out, endlessly repeating the romantic myths. Previously, better-known, more accomplished writers made their names and sometimes their fortunes out of Cornwall. Daphne du Maurier, John Betjeman, EV Thompson and Winston Graham were literary visitors who put Cornwall on the map. Even higher-profile writers such as Tennyson, Thomas Hardy and DH Lawrence had something to say about Cornwall, drawn by romantic longings.

Probably the most powerful longing is provided by the coastal scenery that tempts multitudes westwards. An urge to follow the setting sun and gape at the sea produces the post-modern pilgrimage to Land's End as millions of feet pound the cliff top into dust. Scenic Cornwall is the raw material for the tourist industry which, while only directly employing around one in ten of the workforce, monopolizes representations of Cornwall.

Since 1999 and the advent of the cornucopia of large-scale European grant aid, another image of Cornwall has surfaced. This is 'Quality Cornwall'. Building on long-standing myths, here is a Cornwall more explicitly moulded by public relations industry image-makers. It emphasizes 'cultural' tourism, the 'gourmet coast' and 'lifestyle Cornwall'. This is Cornwall as the place to be in order to 'set yourself free', with a 'great work-life balance' that helps people 'escape the stresses of urban living by heading to the county'. This, the advertising campaign of Cornwall Pure Business, funded by Cornwall Council and the EU, is the latest in a long line of similar attempts to sell Cornwall to others.

Fowey

Fowey is picturesque Cornwall *par excellence*, its houses tumbling down the steep hillside, descending to its deep estuary. Since 1997 it has hosted the annual Daphne du Maurier Festival of Arts & Literature, proudly advertising itself as the 'Best festival in England', and attracting English glitterati from the arts world. With its emphasis on landscape and 'enchanted Cornwall', this festival, like the St Endellion Music Festivals on the North Coast, is a cultural event that, although based on a place, is essentially placeless.

Reflecting its location as a centre of 'cultural' tourism, Fowey has a relatively high proportion of its workforce employed in tourism, and a relatively high number enjoying low pay. Moreover, almost one in five of its properties are holiday and second homes. Indeed, on a measure of community sustainability, Fowey East ranks as the sixth most unsustainable out of the 328 districts in Cornwall.

But there is another side to Fowey, now one of Cornwall's smaller towns. It stole the trade of its up-river rival Lostwithiel during the thirteenth century as the river silted up and ships could no longer reach the quays upstream. In the following century it became a bustling and turbulent port. Fowey then led Cornwall's foray into the surrounding ocean. In 1346 the port provided one of the largest numbers of ships for the English crown to lay siege to Calais. Trading was increasingly supplemented by piracy in the troubled fifteenth century, and by the 1470s the port's mariners were being pursued by the authorities for their 'depredations'. Meanwhile, a French expedition had burnt the town in 1457.

Such excitement, and a reputation for lawlessness – or was it sturdy independence? – had subsided by the beginning of the twentieth century. Largely by-passed by Cornwall's industrialization, Fowey turned into a somewhat sleepy haven, overshadowed by the new seventeenth-century ports of Falmouth and Penzance to the west.

But the place was home to one of Cornwall's greatest writers – Arthur Quiller-Couch, who lived at The Haven near the end of the Bodinnick ferry crossing. Quiller-Couch (1863–1944), or 'Q' as he was widely known, put Fowey well and truly on the literary map with his stories set in 'Troy Town'. Q was much more than a gifted short-story writer, becoming the first Professor of English Literature at Cambridge University, and dividing his time between Fowey and Cambridge.

Q was Cornwall's leading man of letters from the 1890s for half a century, but still found time for public affairs. He edited the influential though short-lived *Cornish Magazine* in 1899–1900, and was prominent in local Liberal Party activities. Though moving in the upper reaches of Cornish society, in the inter-war period Q was ready to lend a hand to local boys with talent, such as the precocious AL Rowse from nearby St Austell (though he failed to detect the promise in Jack Clemo).

The Haven (top left). Streets descend to the deep estuary of Fowey (above and left)

He was also active in the Cornish branch of the Society for the Preservation of Rural England, railing against the developments of the 1930s. However, he was equally sceptical about the parallel Cornish revival, observing drily that at restaged Cornish-language mystery plays the audience would have to do more acting than the actors.

Godrevy Lighthouse

In 2009, when a stretch of Gwithian Towans was up for sale, newspapers the length and breadth of Britain found a ready excuse to plaster photos of Godrevy Lighthouse across their pages. It might not have been very near the land for sale, but it was one of those images that spell 'Cornwall', foaming waves crashing on to rocky shores.

Godrevy Lighthouse is well known as the inspiration of Virginia Woolf's novel *To the Lighthouse*, published in 1927. Ostensibly set in Scotland, the book was triggered by the Woolf family's annual holiday pilgrimage to St Ives. There they stayed near Porthminster Beach, now well known for its beach café that kick-started St Ives' entry into Cornwall's gourmet-coast culture.

The lighthouse itself was built in 1859 to warn mariners of a series of low rocks that threaten any shipping travelling northwards too close to the Iron Age fort of Godrevy Head. To the east, seals come every year to breed. The cliff footpath offers a convenient vantage for human voyeurs. From its edge you can peer down the vertiginous cliffs at the seal colony basking in the sun.

To the west of the lighthouse runs a long beach, once proudly advertised as 'three miles of golden sands', backed by dunes, or 'towans'. The golden sands here actually were (and still are) streaked with black, a lingering reminder of the coal-fired power station that stood at the Hayle end of the towans. The power station and its more short-lived neighbours – a dynamite works and explosives factories – are now just a memory. In their place the plan was to use part of the towans to build yet more houses. This would mirror the new supermarket which has been plonked on Hayle's formerly derelict shipping wharves (below).

The Eden Project

In recent years one of the bestselling non-fiction books in Britain has been a guide to the Eden Project. Its popularity is testament to the number of visitors to this former clay pit, where the domes have become an iconic statement of a confident, brash 'New Cornwall'. They arrived at the end of the 1990s after a life-giving injection of public money when Cornwall was designated as a recipient of Objective One European grant aid – the highest level of financial support available. The Eden Project, along with the new university campus at Tremough near Penryn, was one of the two projects that swallowed the bulk of European funding.

The Eden Project is a Cornish paradox. On the one hand it hosts serious horticultural research work, attracting the support of some of the most respected people in the plants world, and adding greatly to our understanding of the changing world around us. It cleverly combines an exciting tourist attraction with an important educational message, but has not allowed the latter to overpower the visitors' experience. Its very laudable aim is to alert us to the need to change our unsustainable, consumption-obsessed lifestyles.

Yet, on the other hand, it is home to the biggest car-park in Cornwall and triggers thousands of extra car trips to the county, thus helping to increase carbon emissions. It has a programme to help people learn about climate change – the 'Climate Revolution' – and its website admonishes us to reduce our carbon use. Yet one searches in vain for information about its own direct and indirect carbon footprint.

Furthermore, although Eden is one of several aspects of modern Cornwall where healthy criticism is not encouraged, critics point to a contradiction between its green ambitions and its actual impact. Eden is charged by some as indulging in 'greenwash' on a gigantic scale – for example, through entering into partnership with companies such as the French energy giant EDF. Such deals allow the latter to claim green credentials. Similarly, an offsetting agreement with Cornwall Council's Newquay airport allows the Council to feel better about irresponsibly increasing carbon emissions while expecting others (usually in the Global South) to reduce theirs. Such schemes cloak deeply unsustainable practices, and make some wonder whether Eden is actually part of the solution or part of the problem.

Carland Cross
Wind Turbines

The wind turbines that dramatically appear over the brow of the hill as the main A30 rises to Carland Cross roundabout have become in their own way icons of Cornwall. They were among the first wind turbines to be built in the UK, put up in 1992. They've now been joined by several other wind farms, from east of Redruth up to Morwenstow.

Wind turbines, harnessing the constant winds that have buffeted Cornwall and stunted trees for centuries, seem at home here. Cornwall's westerly position, jutting out into the Atlantic, makes it an obvious site for increasing the proportion of energy provided by renewables in the UK, and also promises a greater degree of energy self-sufficiency.

But Cornwall is also part of a small, overcrowded offshore European island. Wind farms inevitably incur protests from nearby residents, and others concerned with their impact on a cherished landscape. As upland areas, the best sites for wind farms are often also sites of special interest, or homes to fragile archaeological relics. Conflicts have already surfaced. Planning permissions for wind turbines at Pensilva, near Liskeard, and on Bodmin Moor were rejected in 2008.

Scottish Power has replaced the original 15 turbines at Carland Cross, in order to double the megawattage. But fewer turbines means bigger turbines and these were origi-

nally planned to be twice as big as the existing ones. As their height became plain, considerable opposition emerged. Permission was originally denied, one of the last acts of the doomed Carrick District Council before it disappeared. The new unitary authority approved a revised scheme. How we square an urgent need for more renewable energy with entrenched attitudes to our landscape, and resistance from those who live near them, is an enigma that the 'one size fits all' Cornwall Council still has to resolve.

Places to Visit

With the exception of Lanherne Manor, the places featured in this book may be visited or viewed from the outside, many without charge. A number of organizations have collections of related interest.

China Clay Country Park
Wheal Martyn
Carthew
St Austell PL26 8XG
Tel: 01726 850362
www. wheal-martyn.com

The Delabole Slate Quarry
Pengelly
Delabole PL33 9AZ
Tel: 01840 212242
www. delaboleslate.co.uk

Goonhilly Visitor Centre
Helston TR12 6LQ
Tel: 0800 679593
Email: goonhilly.visitorscentre@bt.com
www.goonhilly.bt.com

Geevor Tin Mine Museum
Pendeen
Penzance TR19 7EW
Tel: 01736 788662
www.geevor.com

Hayle Heritage Centre
John Harvey House
24 Foundry Square
Hayle TR27 4HH
www.hayleheritagecentre.org.uk

Penlee House Gallery & Museum
Morrab Road
Penzance TR18 4HE
Tel: 01736 363625
Email: info@penleehouse.org.uk
www. penleehouse.org.uk

Porthcurno Telegraph Museum
Porthcurno TR19 6JX
Tel: 01736 810966
www.porthcurno.org.uk

Royal Cornwall Museum
River Street
Truro TR1 2SJ
Tel: 01872 272205
Email: enquiries@royalcornwallmuseum.org.uk
www.royalcornwallmuseum.org.uk

Cornwall Museums has a portal providing links to more than 50 museums in Cornwall, at **www.museumsincornwall.org.uk**.